LOOKING AT PATRONAGE

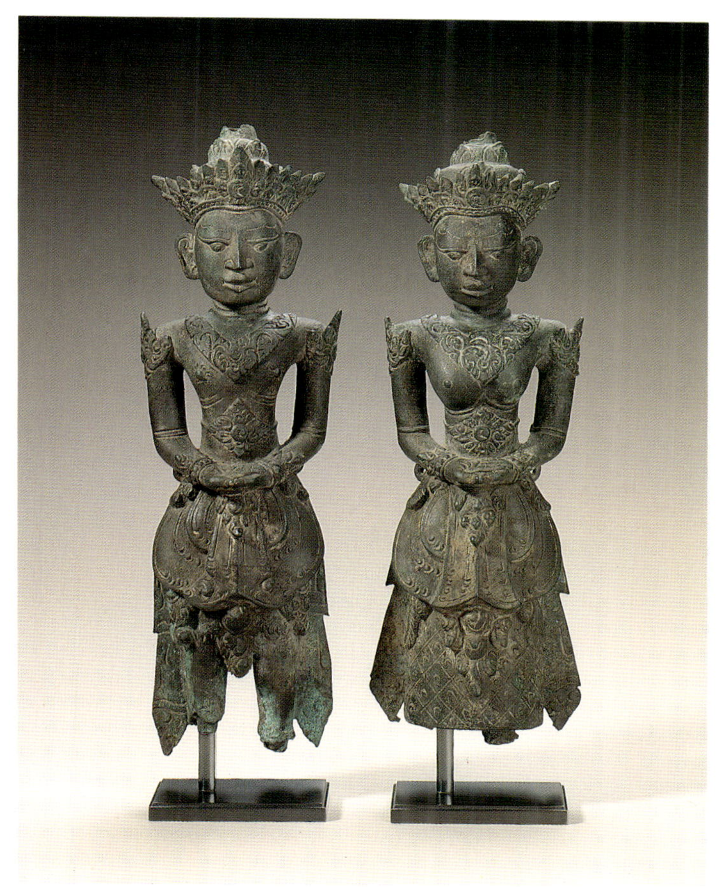

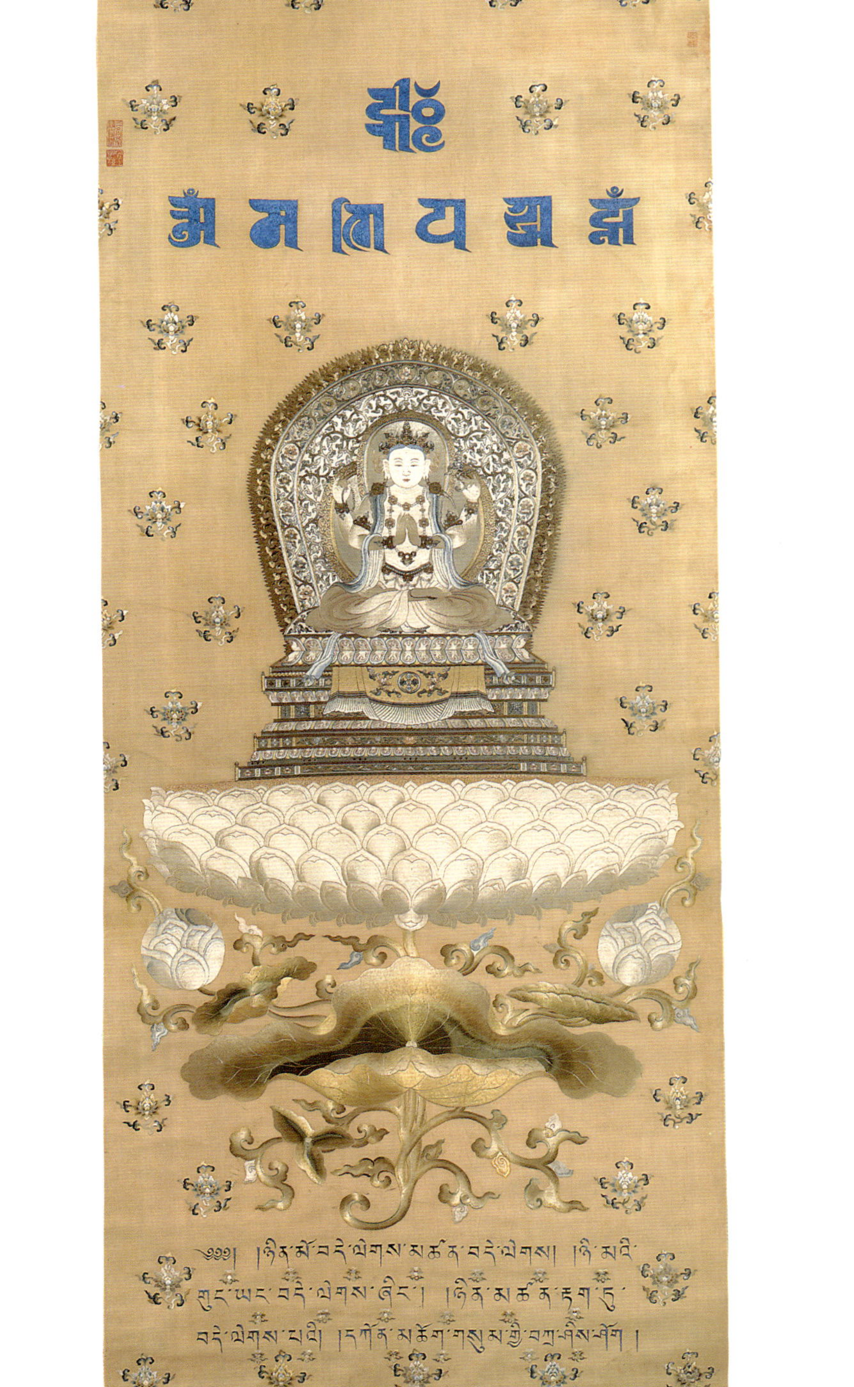
༄༅། །ཉིན་མོ་བདེ་ལེགས་མཚན་བདེ་ལེགས། །ཉི་མའི་
གུང་ཡང་བདེ་ལེགས་ཞིང་། །ཉིན་མཚན་རྟག་ཏུ་
བདེ་ལེགས་པའི། །དཀོན་མཆོག་གསུམ་གྱི་བཀྲ་ཤིས་ཤོག །

LOOKING AT PATRONAGE

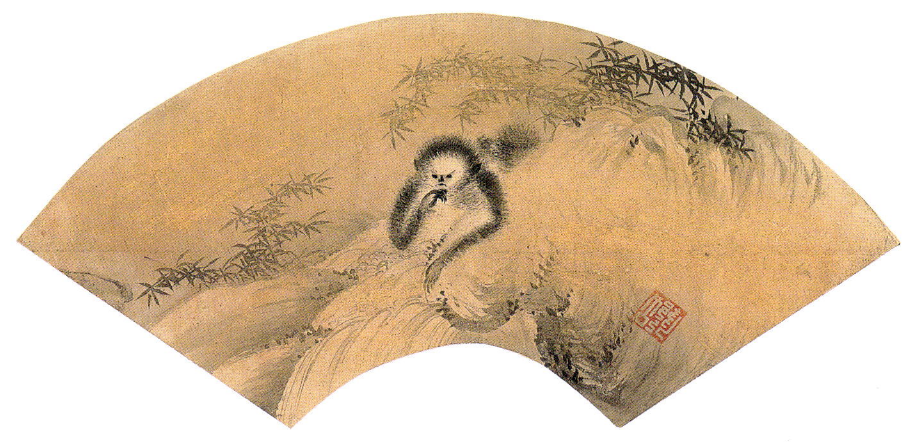

RECENT ACQUISITIONS OF ASIAN ART

ASIAN ART MUSEUM OF SAN FRANCISCO
1989

Published by
Asian Art Museum of San Francisco
Golden Gate Park
San Francisco, CA 94118

ISBN 0-939117-03-7

LC89-80817

Cover: *The Path through Mount Utsu* (detail), by Fukae Roshū (1699–1757). Japan; Edo period. (Cat. no. 48)

Back cover: *Wheeled Cart with Two Jars on Perforated Stand*. Korea; Three Kingdoms period, Kaya, 5th–6th century. (Cat. no. 38)

Half-title: *Funerary Figures*. Bali, Indonesia; 15th–16th century. (Cat. no. 22)

Frontispiece: *Bodhisattva Avalokiteshvara*. China; Qing dynasty, Qianlong mark and period (1736–1795). (Cat. no. 32)

Title page: *Monkey*, by Shikibu Terutada (fl. mid-16th century). Japan; Muromachi period. (Cat. no. 42)

Publication Coordinator: So Kam Ng
Publication Assistants: Rex Faubion and Elizabeth Ingalls
Editor: Lorna Price
Design and Production: Ed Marquand Book Design
Photography: Kaz Tsuruta, Joseph McDonald, James M. Medley
Typesetting: Centerpoint/Type Gallery, Inc., Seattle
Printing: Dai Nippon Printing Co., Ltd., Tokyo

Printed and bound in Japan

TABLE OF CONTENTS

PREFACE

Most great artists and cultural institutions have flourished through the ages under the patronage of individuals of means. The patrons of the past were not only the kings and courtiers of history and legend; eventually, far more numerous were those patrons much like ourselves: private individuals, merchants, scholars, poets, writers, civic leaders, institutions of the state and the city. Such were, and are, the patrons represented by the works of art that it is our present privilege to cherish, preserve, and display in the Asian Art Museum of the City of San Francisco.

Patronage of the arts is a noble passion, one shared over the course of centuries by men and women of discrimination, taste, and foresight. Spurred by their love of the arts, today's patrons, through their benefactions, continue to add immeasurably to the general well-being of the society they serve. Public museums, a relatively late form of high patronage, are perhaps the grandest manifestation of enlightened support for the visual arts. American museums shine brightest in this century's cultural firmament; we have been fortunate beyond all others in having the greatest and most dedicated of patrons.

Occasionally there occurs a perfect union in the arts between an individual and a municipality. Acting in concert, the private citizen and the city create an entity that is devoted to the perpetual enrichment of the populace. Such is the extraordinary case of the Asian Art Museum of San Francisco. There is no question that this museum's two great patrons have been Avery Brundage and the City of San Francisco. While other patrons may have been able to spend more on collecting, no one had a better eye than Mr. Brundage for works of Asian art. In the City of San Francisco, Avery Brundage found not only a highly motivated collaborator but also a city linked to Asia by many bonds. Certainly no other city could have provided this uniquely appropriate setting for a museum devoted to all the arts of Asia. This exhibition is presented, first, to honor these two foremost patrons.

The exhibition is also a tribute to those historical patrons, individuals and institutions, known and unknown, who originally commissioned the art now in our museum. It is no less a tribute to today's patrons. Having been well established a generation ago, this museum thrives now by the continuing generosity of those who have taken their example from its founders. We grow by their enthusiasm for the arts, and it is likely that we will always, to a significant extent, depend upon their kindness. They continue to make it possible for San Francisco to hold great Asian art, for the benefit of all.

The theme for the exhibition was first suggested by scholar-patron Emma Bunker. Mrs. Bunker founded and now chairs our Connoisseur's Council, the generous association working within the museum, which has enabled us to acquire many outstanding works. I thank the Connoisseur's Council for their excellent efforts on behalf of the museum as well as the Asian Art Commission and its chairman, Alice Lowe, and the board of the Asian Art Museum Foundation and its chairman, Judith F. Wilbur. This outstanding core of volunteers works closely with our staff of dedicated curators and administrators to make the museum a vital part of America's cultural life.

This exhibition was directed by Chief Curator Clarence Shangraw. An outstanding scholar of Chinese ceramics, he is among the few individuals at the museum to have had the pleasure of working directly with Mr. Brundage. In an important sense, this exhibition also honors Mr. Shangraw, for it marks his twenty-fifth anniversary with our institution. We are pleased and proud to dedicate this catalogue to Clarence Shangraw in honor of his signal contribution to the Asian Art Museum.

Rand Castile
Director

PATRONS

Looking at Patronage, the catalogue of an exhibition at the Asian Art Museum in the fall of 1989, has been made possible by:

The Society for Asian Art

Shawn and Brook Byers
Richard Gump

Mr. and Mrs. Johnson S. Bogart
Mr. and Mrs. Courtney J. Catron
Mr. and Mrs. Stuart G. Moldaw
Margaret Polak
Walter and Phyllis Shorenstein
Mrs. Virginia Lee Taylor
Mr. and Mrs. M. Glenn Vinson, Jr.

CONTRIBUTING SCHOLARS

Terese Tse Bartholomew, *Curator of Indian and Himalayan Art*
Patricia Berger, *Curator of Chinese Art*
Rand Castile, *Director*
Nancy Hock, *Paul L. and Phyllis Wattis Foundation Curator of Southeast Asian Art*
Yoshiko Kakudo, *Curator of Japanese Art*
Kumja Paik Kim, *Associate Curator of Korean Art*
Richard Mellott, *Curator of Education*
So Kam Ng, *Associate Curator of Education*
Clarence F. Shangraw, *Chief Curator*
Yoko Woodson, *Associate Curator of Japanese Art*
Terry Allen, *Historian of Islamic Art*, Sebastopol

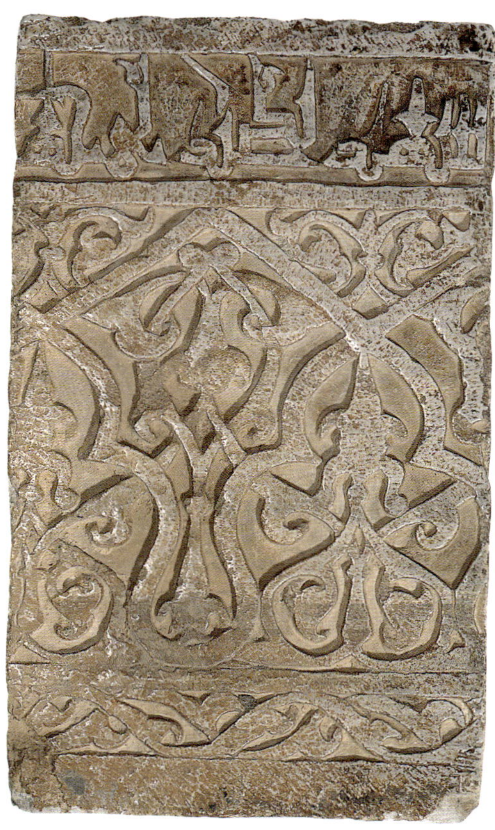

1. MARBLE DADO PANEL WITH PERSIAN INSCRIPTION AND ARABESQUE

Afghanistan; from the Palace of Sultan Mas'ud III (r. 1099–1115), Ghazni; 1112
H: 74.2 cm (29¼ in.) W: 43.1 cm (17 in.)
87 S3
Gift of Shawn and Brook Byers, and Peter Marks in honor of Avery Brundage's Centenary Year

'Ala' al-Daulah Mas'ud III (b. 1061) was the twelfth ruler of the Ghaznavid dynasty founded by Turkish mercenaries in 977. Ghazni in northeastern Afghanistan was its capital and quickly became a cultural magnet; there, around 1000, the great Persian poet Firdausi composed his version of the national epic, the *Shāh namah*, in Persian. By Mas'ud III's day the dynasty was in decline, but the Ghaznavids still raided into northwestern India, as they had done for well over a century. Ghazni was sacked in 1150, and the dynasty ended in 1186. Ghaznavid monuments still dot the ruins of the old city, among them a famous minaret built by Mas'ud III.

This panel is part of a marble dado that was wrapped around the arcade piers of the central courtyard of the palace of Mas'ud III. The Italian excavators of the site established that when complete the dado comprised over 500 such panels and totaled 250 meters in length; the courtyard itself measures approximately 50 by 32 meters. Of the original ensemble, only forty-four panels were found in situ. An Arabic inscription found in the palace dates it to 1112–1113 and gives the name of the presumed architect, Muhammad b. Husayn b. Mubarak (otherwise unknown). This dado panel, the only complete example known to exist outside Afghanistan, had been reused elsewhere in Ghazni.

The dado is of particular interest for the Persian inscription it bears, even though each panel carries only a few words, and most of the dado is lost.[1] But from what remains, it is clear that the inscription is part of a poem eulogizing the ancestors of Mas'ud III and describing his works. It was probably written by the court poet Mas'ud-i S'ad-i Salman specifically to celebrate the palace in which it appeared.[2]

Its main significance, though, is that it is one of the earliest extant examples of the use of Persian for a monumental inscription. After the Arab Islamic conquest in the seventh century, Persian came to be written in Arabic characters, but it stood in the same subordinate relationship to Arabic as did the vernacular languages of medieval Europe to Latin. Formal inscriptions like this one continued to be executed in Arabic. The community of Ghazni was highly conscious of the status of the Persian language, and this panel is testimony to its emergence, under Turkish patronage, as a high literary language in the eastern Persian-speaking world.

The dado inscription originally was painted in ultramarine blue against a red background, a common scheme in Islamic architecture of the time. This color scheme likely extended to the entire surface of the panel. The main zone of decoration is a frieze of two sets of overlapping trefoil arches, under which abstract vegetation intertwines in a well-developed arabesque closed at top and bottom and with vertical axes corresponding to those of the arches. The lower band is carved with one of the many antique border designs that survive in Islamic art.

The marble from which the panel was cut comes from a nearby quarry. It is the earliest extant example in the Islamic East of the use of marble instead of carved plaster for decorative facing. —T.A. and C.F.S.

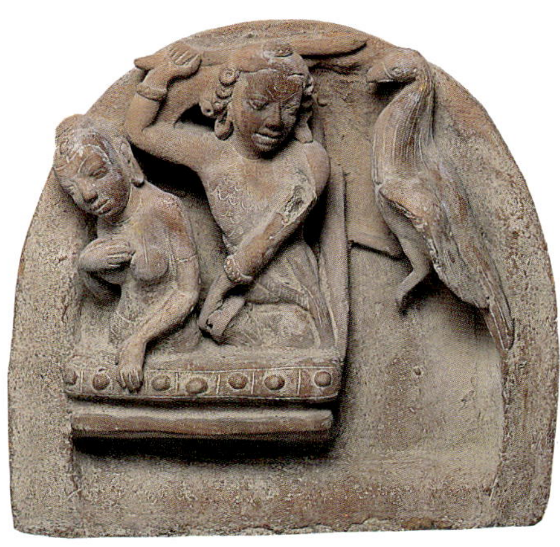

2. RAMAYANA SCENE

Uttar Pradesh, India; Gupta period, 5th century
Terra cotta
H: 40.6 cm (16 in.) W: 41.9 cm (16½ in.)
1988.40
Gift of the Connoisseur's Council

With eloquent gesture and great narrative economy, this relief depicts the fight between the demon king Ravana and Jatayu, king of the vultures. This episode is from the *Ramayana*, the epic dealing with the abduction of Sita, wife of Rama, by the demon Ravana, and the war that ensues. The scene shows Ravana abducting Sita in his chariot on the way to his citadel on the island of Lanka. Jatayu, a devotee of Rama, comes to Sita's rescue, descending upon Ravana with his talons. Sita turns pathetically from the battle, right hand shielding her breast, the left hanging limply, while Ravana, his demonic nature emphasized by his arching eyebrows and bulging eyes, slashes away with his sword. Drama, pathos, anger, and heroism appear in this work. According to the story, Jatayu was no match for Ravana and died in the attempt, but he survived long enough to tell Rama of Sita's whereabouts.

Although this episode of the *Ramayana* is an important and beloved one because of the feeling of devotion (*bhakti*) it conveyed, it is seldom encountered in Indian sculpture.[1] This terra-cotta plaque once ornamented an unknown Gupta temple somewhere in Uttar Pradesh. It was customary to decorate the outside niches of temples with terra-cotta or stone sculptures of this type. This example would have been one of a series of terra-cotta plaques illustrating scenes from the *Ramayana*. Also from the same site is the example in the Rockefeller collection showing Rama seated in conversation with his brother Lakshmana, also an episode from the *Ramayana*.[2] These two examples are similar in style and shape, both having an arched top and figures in high relief. From the subject matter, the temple would have been a Hindu one, possibly dedicated to the worship of Vishnu. The patronage of this terra-cotta relief is uncertain. This work has twice been dated by thermoluminescence technique by Oxford University, and both times the dating has been consistent with the result, i.e., between 1150 and 1800 years ago. —T. T. B.

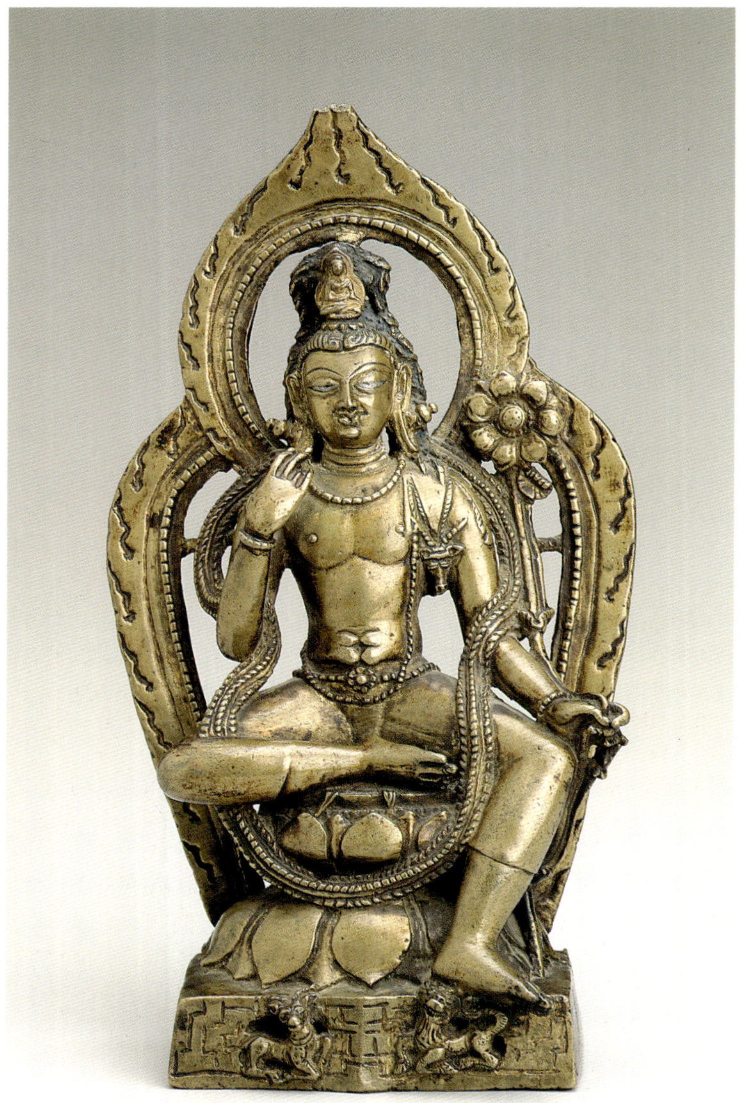

3. SEATED PADMAPANI

Kashmir, India; 11th–12th century
Brass with silver inlay
H: 24.2 cm (9 1/2 in.) W: 13.0 cm (5 1/8 in.)
86 B4
Gift of the LEF Foundation

In India and elsewhere, Buddhist images such as this were usually consecrated in the hope that the donor or donors would acquire spiritual merit for themselves and their families as well as for all sentient beings. Sometimes images were cast as an act of thanksgiving, or to increase one's wealth or longevity. They were kept on personal altars or given to monasteries as pious gifts. Unless the image is inscribed, it is impossible to know the identities of the donor or sculptor.

Padmapani is a form of Avalokiteshvara, the lord of compassion, who holds the most important position in the pantheon of Mahayana Buddhist divinities. He is the "all seeing lord" who saves all sentient beings from peril. As a result, images of Avalokiteshvara in his various forms became very popular from the Gupta period on, second only to that of Buddha.

Padmapani sits in *lalitasana*, with one leg bent and the other leg pendant, on a double lotus throne above a rectangular base. The plain and broad lotus petals are typical of the art of Kashmir, as is the base incised with abstract lines representing a rocky landscape with caves inhabited by two animals.

Padmapani's hair is dressed in a tall crown and ornamented with a seated image of his spiritual father, Amitabha. His right hand is turned toward his face in a contemplative gesture, while his left, resting on his knee, holds the long stem of a full-blown lotus. This flower is his most distinctive attribute; hence his name Padmapani, Lotus-Bearer. Padmapani wears a plain lower garment. His upper torso is bare, draped with an antelope skin (a symbol for ascetics) and a long garland. His typical Kashmiri face has full cheeks, a curved nose, large lotus-petal-shaped eyes inlaid with silver, and a prominent chin. Other Kashmiri characteristics are seen in the naturalistic modeling of the pectoral and abdominal muscles, the beaded aureoles, and the flaming nimbus with typical zig-zag incisions.

By the seventh century, Kashmir was an important center for Buddhist studies. The Chinese monk Xuancang spent two years studying Buddhism in Kashmir. It was to Kashmir that the Tibetan king Tsongtsengampo sent his emissaries in the seventh century, when he wanted an alphabet for his country.[1] Because of its northern location, Kashmir drew its artistic inspiration not only from India but also from the various countries of central Asia. This mixture brought forth an interesting style, which greatly influenced the art styles of Western Tibet and China.[2]

The presence of Kashmiri bronzes in public or private collections in the West is a recent phenomenon. A group of bronzes made its first appearance shortly after the abdication of the Maharaja of Kashmir and his retirement to Bombay in 1948. More bronzes emerged in the 1950s, this time brought to light by political upheavals in Tibet and the resulting exodus of Tibetan refugees to the Western world.[3]—T. T. B.

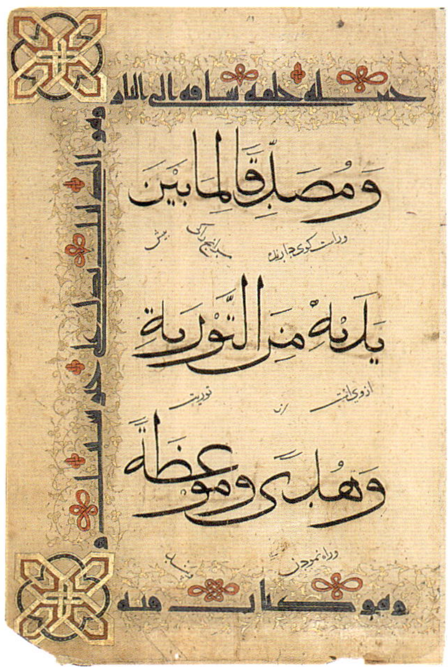

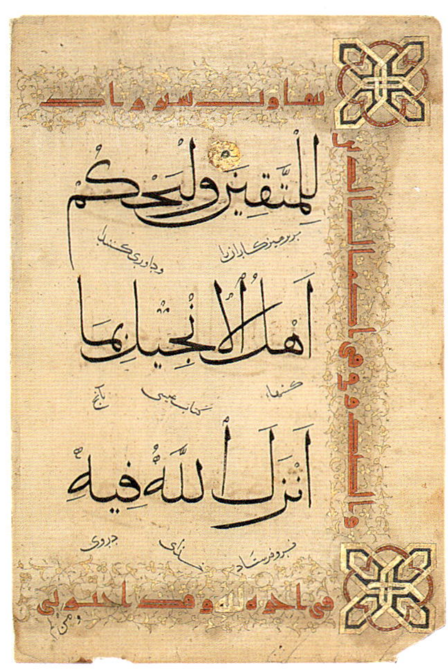

4. ILLUMINATED PAGE FROM A HOLY QUR'AN

North India; Pre-Mughal Delhi Sultanate, 15th century
Black ink, colors, and gold on paper
H: 28.3 cm (11⅜ in.) W: 18.4 cm (7¼ in.)
87 D7
Gift of the Todd G. Williams Memorial Fund
and The Society for Asian Art

This illuminated page of Islamic calligraphy (illustrated front and back), extremely rare for its type and period, comes from a now widely dispersed manuscript of the Holy Qur'an,[1] the text revered among Muslims as God's revelations through Muhammad to humanity. This passage comes from Sura V, verse 46:

> But why do they come
> To thee for decision,
> When they have [their own]
> Law before them?—
> Therein is the [plain]
> Command of God; yet
> Even after that, they would
> Turn away. For they
> Are not [really]
> People of Faith.
> —trans. by A. Yusuf Ali

The anonymous scribe placed three compositionally balanced lines of Arabic on each page in an elegantly flowing *rayhani* script, one of several cursive scripts ideally suited to capture the design versatility of written Arabic. Directly beneath these holy words is the Persian translation and added commentary, styled in Kūfic script. The original owner of this Qur'an was apparently more familiar with Persian than Arabic, a perfectly understandable situation for fifteenth-century India, where the Muslims were Persian.

Calligraphy as practiced throughout the Islamic world combines the power of the sacred word and the rhythmic beauty of the written word. Associated with this art form was the practice of illumination—decorating and gilding in brilliant colors. The elaborate design of this page's surface demonstrates a fascination with geometry, while its richness propagates the integrity of the sacred text.

The illuminated border decoration consists of a large interlocking geometric design in blue, gold, and red at the top and bottom corners, and a delicately composed but sinuously strong arabesque of scrolling leafy vines in gold, linking the corner designs. Over these gold vegetal spirals are lively patterned, randomly placed knots in vibrant reds, while a band of angular Kūfic script, painted in a majestic blue, serves as an inner margin to mark the confines of the illuminated border from the large central area holding the calligraphy.

While calligraphy was a widely practiced art form in literate society during the Delhi sultanate, the lavish illumination of this stately page indicates that it was commissioned by a wealthy patron, most likely one of the sultans recognized as great patrons of the arts, employing a first-rate calligrapher and illuminator. Unfortunately, the colophon of this manuscript, which would have identified the scribe, patron, illuminator, and place of production, has not been located. —C.F.S.

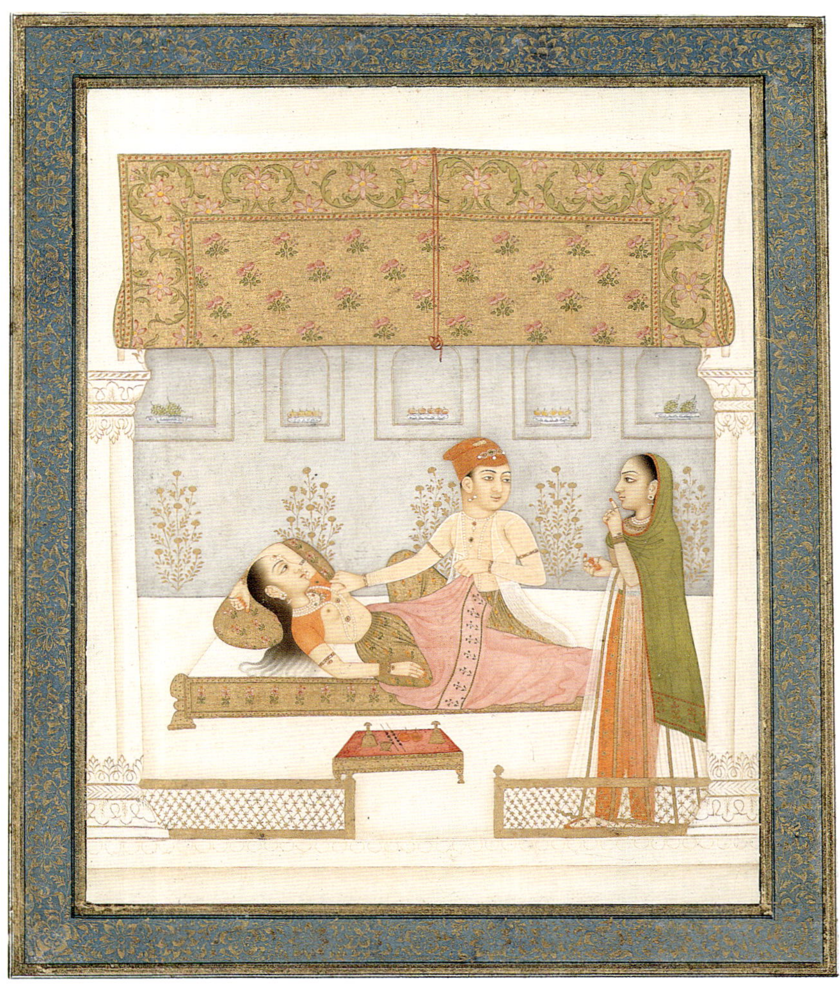

5. A GIRL WOKEN BY A PRINCE

From an album of the Bibliotheca Phillippica,
Warren Hastings Collection
Lucknow, India; 2nd half of 18th century
Colors on paper
H: 17.4 cm (6⁷/₈ in.) W: 14.4 cm (5¹¹/₁₆ in.)
1988.51.24
Gift of George Hopper Fitch

A prince awakens his beloved by fondling her breast and lifting her thin covering. The girl, reclining on a bolster on an elaborate bed, is fully awake; her attendant unsuccessfully tries to restrain the prince with a gesture. The scene takes place in a stark white marble palace between two marble columns and beneath a rolled-up golden blind decorated with pink flowers. The figures stand out against the gray back wall. The five niches in the wall contain fresh fruit in blue-and-white containers; below the niches are floral motifs painted in gold. The use of white marble as a background and the exquisite brushwork are characteristic of Mughal paintings from Oudh (Lucknow).

This superb painting once belonged to Warren Hastings (1732–1818), the first governor general of India. An enlightened man, Hastings promoted and encouraged Oriental studies. He was also a great patron of art. Not only did he help European artists newly arrived in India, he also commissioned and collected Indian miniature paintings, and encouraged his contemporaries to do the same. His collection was dispersed after his death, and its full extent is not known other than a few stray miniatures and the album purchased by Sir Thomas Phillips (1792–1872) at the Daylesford sale in 1853.[1] This album is also dispersed.[2]

Another Mughal painting in the museum's collection, also given by Mr. Fitch, came from the same album collected originally by Warren Hastings and then by Thomas Phillips. Both paintings share the same gilt-sprinkled margin, with an inner blue border painted with gold flowers. — T. T. B.

6. IDEALIZED HEAD OF A WOMAN

Rajasthan, India; Kishangarh school, mid-18th century
Ink and color on paper
H: 31.1 cm (12¼ in.) W: 22.8 cm (9 in.)
1988.23.1
Gift of Dr. William K. Ehrenfeld

The development of miniature painting in India is closely linked with patronage. The early Mughal emperors brought the art of miniature painting from Persia to India. They were great patrons of art; artists flocked to their courts, and painting reached great heights during their reign. However, from the reign of Aurangzeb on (1658–1707), the emphasis was not on commissioning painting but on protecting the empire. A kind of cultural exodus soon began, as artists left the Mughal court in search of patrons elsewhere. During the seventeenth and eighteenth centuries, the princes of Rajasthan became quite affluent through trade. Some, imitating the Mughal courts, had their own ateliers and thus attracted many Mughal court artists. Their style of painting soon merged with local styles; as a result, the art of painting flourished in Rajasthan during the seventeenth and eighteenth centuries.

The small state of Kishangarh, founded in 1611, lies in the middle of Rajasthan between Jaipur and Ajmer. From the seventeenth through the nineteenth centuries, the courts of Kishangarh supported scores of artists. By the mid-eighteenth century, the distinctive style of Kishangarh had evolved. It is characterized by lean and elegant, elongated human figures with typical arching eyebrows and lotus-petal-shaped eyes.

This portrait, rendered in elegant brushwork, is lightly tinted with washes. The woman is beautifully coiffed and bejeweled, her elaborate hairdo further embellished by strings of pearls and fresh rosebuds. The strong profile is softened by subtle shadings and the soft cascading hair. The arching eyebrows and the lotus eye tinged with pink are characteristic of the Kishangarh style.

This idealized study of a woman is based on Mughal prototypes. During the eighteenth century such portraits were popular. Mughal artists often painted female portraits in profile, because a frontal view "implied all-too-audacious friendliness on the part of the sitter."[1] — T. T. B.

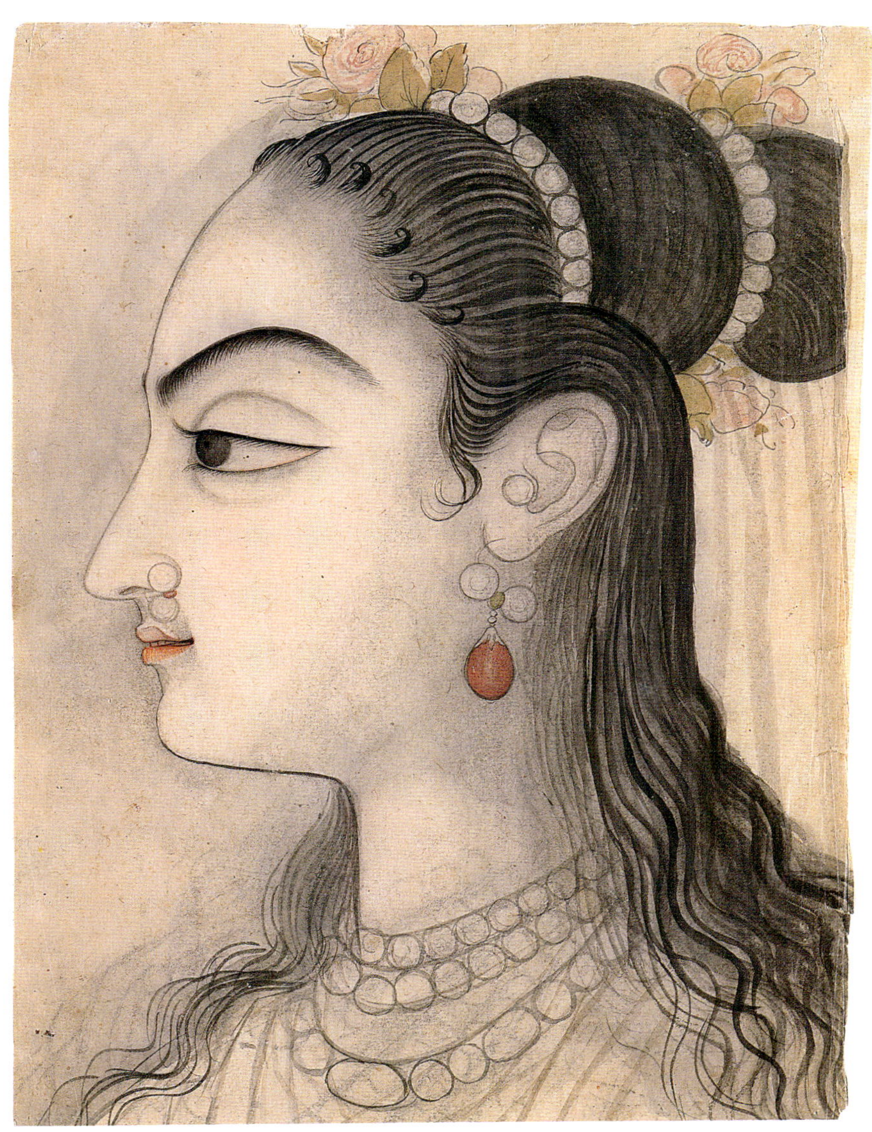

7. LADY HOLDING FLOWERS

Rajasthan, India; Kishangarh school, ca. 1750–1775
Colors on paper
H: 33.6 cm (13¼ in.) W: 26.0 cm (10¼ in.)
87 D27
Gift of the Collection of Gursharan and Elvira Sidhu

This painting from the royal Kishangarh collection depicts a young lady standing alone in a vast green landscape with a high horizon. Thin-waisted, her body elongated, she stands with a slight arch to her back, holding a lotus in her left hand and a branch of small blossoms in her right. (During the monsoon season, many pink lotuses bloom in the lakes of Kishangarh. The blossom is often depicted in Kishangarh painting.) She is sumptuously bejeweled. Her transparent, gauzelike skirt reveals a long pink undergarment ornamented with golden motifs. Her face is elongated, with a receding forehead and a pointed chin. She is depicted with a sharp, pointed nose, arching eyebrows, and a lotus-petal-shaped, upcurving eye. Her facial features are strongly reminiscent of those of Radha (the favorite milkmaid of Krishna) painted by Nihal Chand, the foremost court painter of Savant Singh of Kishangarh.[1]

The greatest patron of art among the Kishangarh rulers was Savant Singh, who reigned from 1748–1757. Like the rajas before him, Savant Singh was a devotee of the god Krishna. He was also a poet who wrote under the pseudonym Nagaridas and was noted for his devotional poetry to Krishna. He fell in love with the beautiful and accomplished Bani Thani, a maidservant to his stepmother. Bani Thani became Savant Singh's mistress, and she was supposed to be the model and inspiration for Nihal Chand's portrayal of Radha.[2]

Nihal Chand was famous for his unsurpassed depictions of Krishna and Radha. His figures are thin and elongated, and their facial features are very similar to those of the young lady described above. Nihal Chand is assumed to have developed the iconic portraiture for Krishna and Radha, and their facial characteristics became the standard for Kishangarh painting from then on.

Savant Singh abdicated in 1757, and Bani Thani accompanied him to Brindaban (the center of Krishna worship), where he spent his remaining years as a devotee of Krishna. Nihal Chand remained in Kishangarh and continued to paint under the patronage of the Kishangarh rajas.[3] —T. T. B.

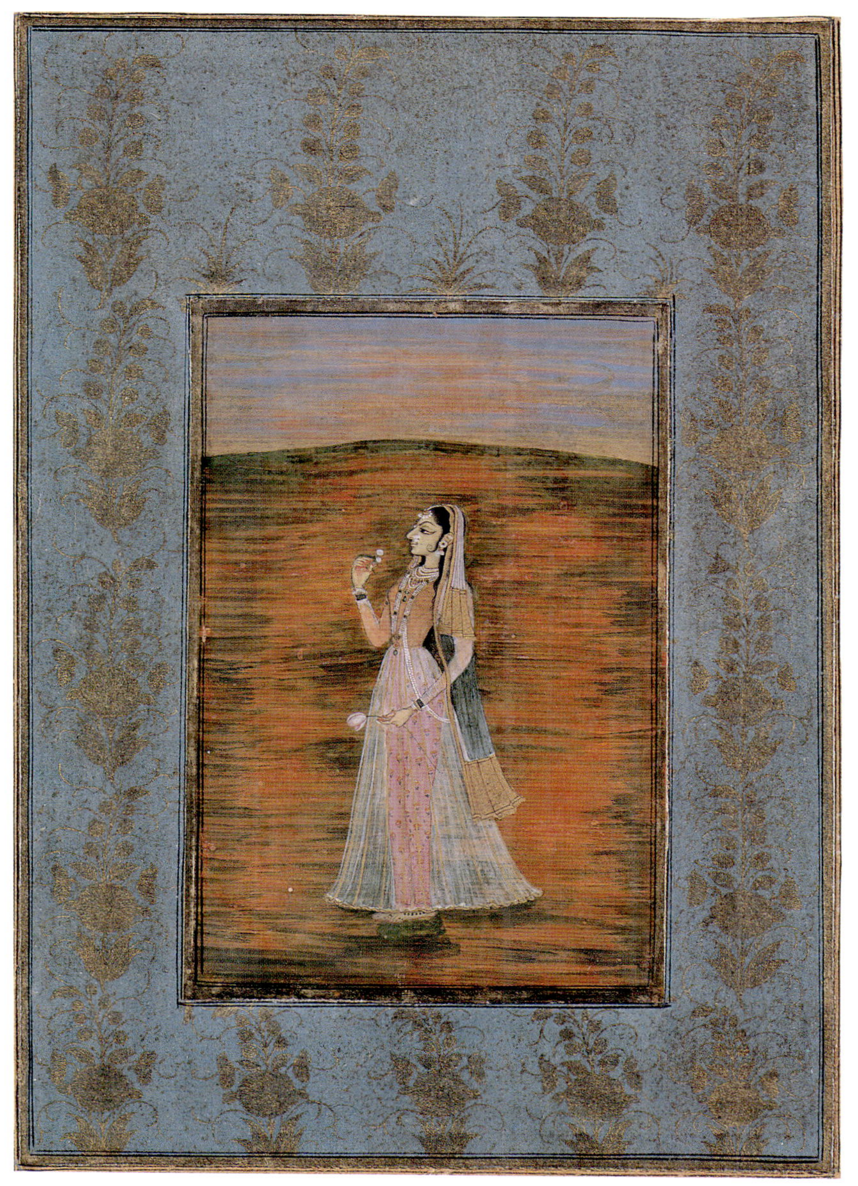

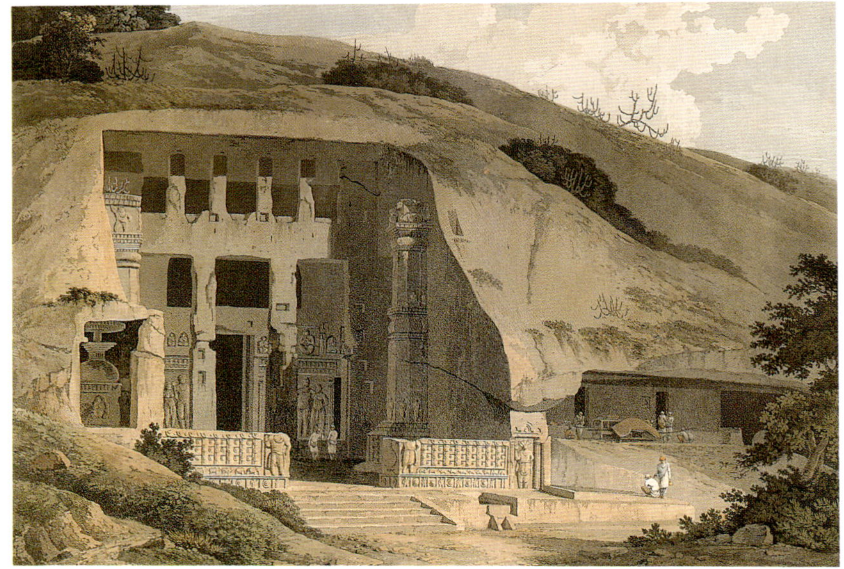

8. AN EXCAVATED TEMPLE ON THE ISLAND OF SALSETTE

From *Antiquities of India*, by Thomas and William Daniell
India; December 1799
Colored aquatint
H: 42.5 cm (16¾ in.) W: 60.3 cm (23¾ in.)
86 D20.16
Gift of Richard B. Gump

Thomas Daniell (1749–1840) and his nephew William (1769–1837) were British artists famous for their landscape paintings and renditions of Indian scenes in aquatint. Inspired by tales of successful British artists who worked in India in the late eighteenth century, Thomas Daniell, then little known, decided to seek his fortune in India. He applied as an engraver to the East India Company and left for India in 1785 with young William.

The Daniells were unsurpassed draftsmen, hard workers as well as artists endowed with business acumen. Thomas and his nephew lost no time in producing a set of twelve views of Calcutta executed in aquatint, a printmaking process invented in the late eighteenth century. The Daniells held a lottery for their works in Calcutta, and with the proceeds they left for Central and Northern India. They traveled to many little-known areas, and everywhere they went, they sketched. Returning to Calcutta with 150 sketches, they again held a lottery and with the proceeds went to Madras in Southern India. By this method the Daniells continued to finance their many trips on the subcontinent.

This print depicts the famous rock-cut *chaitya* (assembly hall) of Kanheri, situated about 20 miles north of Bombay. This impressive *chaitya* is also noted for its inscriptions, which indicate that it was dedicated during the reign of Yajnasri Satakarni, the last great Satavahana ruler, who reigned about the latter part of the second century. This scene was sketched during the Daniells' journey in Bombay (1793–1794), their last sojourn in India. There they met the artist James Wales, who was very interested in the cave temples of Western India. Wales took the Daniells to Elephanta, Kanheri, and various other caves on Salsette Island.

Returning to England in 1794, the Daniells rendered some of their sketches as aquatints; this print was part of their *Oriental Scenery* series, produced between 1795 and 1808. The Daniell prints were very popular in both England and India. While the British in India purchased these prints for their libraries or to decorate their homes, offices, and clubs, the English at home collected the Daniell prints because of their romantic depiction of the Indian subcontinent, the "jewel in the crown." Their exotic and picturesque quality also appealed to other collectors interested in antiquities.

The popularity of the Daniell prints inspired contemporary architecture in England, such as the aviary at the Brighton Pavilion. The prints also appeared as decorations on Staffordshire porcelains as well as on French wallpaper.[1] —T. T. B.

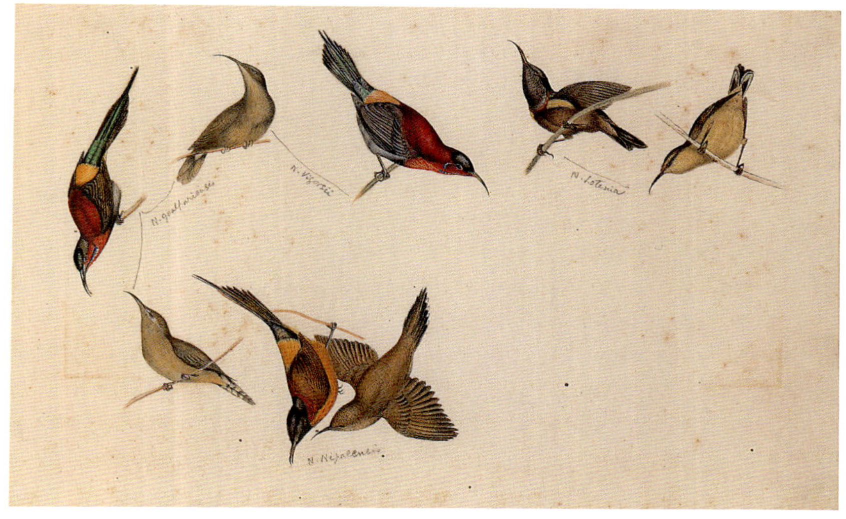

9. SUNBIRDS

India; Company school, mid-19th century
Watercolor on paper
H: 18.4 cm (7¼ in.) W: 29.2 cm (11½ in.)
1988.22
Gift of Mr. and Mrs. Willard G. Clark

"Company school" is an art historical term coined by Indian scholars to describe a special type of Indian painting commissioned by the British in the eighteenth and nineteenth centuries to illustrate life in India. According to Mildred Archer, the leading authority on the Company school, "This painting was mainly a product of the British connection, and despite many local differences of manner, it illustrated a single phenomenon—an attempt by Indian artists to adjust their styles to British needs and to paint subjects of British appeal."[1]

Besides the architecture and scenery of India, the British also showed a keen interest in the flora and fauna of the subcontinent, especially during the late eighteenth and the whole of the nineteenth century. Not only did they collect specimens, they also procured drawings and paintings of birds, animals, and plants. This enthusiasm for the study of natural history was shared by British residents, travelers, and the officers of the East India Company. Members of the Company were especially encouraged to take an interest in recording the animals and plants they encountered, in order to have a better knowledge of the resources of India.

The majority of these natural history paintings were done by Indian artists. Because of the political situation in the late eighteenth century, Mughal patronage weakened, and many Indian artists lost their means of livelihood. Some of these well-trained artists flocked to Calcutta, Tanjore, and Madras to seek work among the British community, and they were willing to accept any job, however menial. Lady Impey, wife of the Chief Justice of the Supreme Court in Calcutta, was known to have employed at least three painters to paint birds, mammals, insects, and flowers in large format between 1774 and 1782.[2]

This work is a fine study of several species of sunbirds of the genera *Nectarinia* and *Aethopyga.*[3] Commonly seen in India, these small songbirds, old-world equivalents of hummingbirds, have brilliant and iridescent feathers and feed largely on nectar. The workmanship is excellent and sensitive and shows a close observation of nature. The Latin names for the four pairs of sunbirds have been written in pencil. Using the currently accepted nomenclature, they are, starting from the upper right, *Nectarinia lotenia,* or Loten's sunbird; *Aethopyga siparaja vigorsii* (*N. vigorsii*) or crimson sunbird; *Aethopyga siparaja seheriae* (*N. goalpariensis*), a subspecies of crimson sunbird; and *N. nipalensis*, or green-tailed sunbird. —T. T. B.

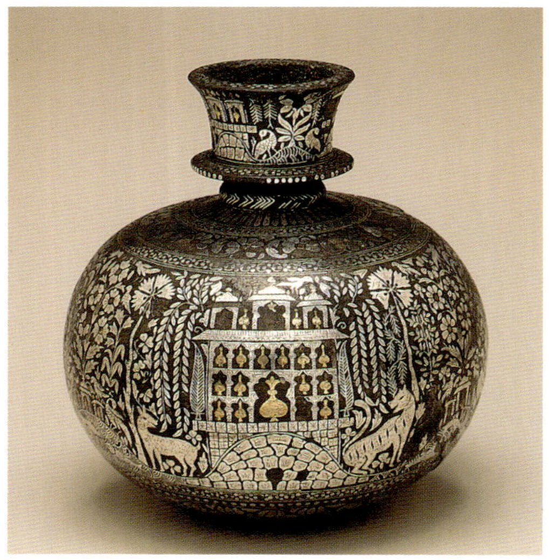

10. HUQQA BASE

Deccan, India; late 17th century
Bidri ware, alloy with silver and brass inlay
H: 18.5 cm (7 1/4 in.)
86 M11
Gift of Marjorie Bissinger Seller

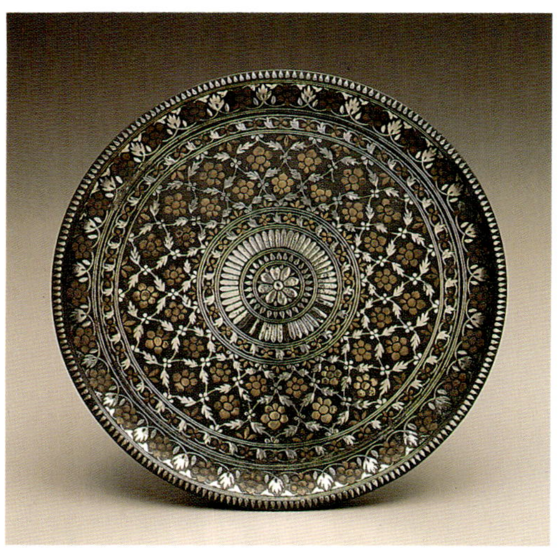

11. PLATE

Deccan, India; 17th–18th century
Bidri ware, alloy with silver and brass inlay
Diam: 19.0 cm (7 1/2 in.)
86 M12
Gift of Martha Davidson in memory of J. LeRoy Davidson

Although the origin of Bidri ware is uncertain, it is named for Bidar, a city in the Deccan that produced such wares in the seventeenth century. There is no doubt that Bidri ware is related to the metalwork of the Islamic world; the technique, however, is truly Indian and is not found elsewhere.

Bidri pieces are cast from an alloy consisting mainly of zinc and small amounts of lead, copper, and tin. Zinc, a soft metal, can be engraved easily; the engraved areas are then inlaid with silver, copper, brass, and occasionally gold. After the inlay is burnished, the vessel is coated with a paste of ammonium chloride, potassium nitrate, sodium chloride, copper sulphate, and mud, which gives the body its characteristic dark appearance but has no effect on the inlay. To darken the surface even further, oil is rubbed into the piece after the paste has been washed off. The beauty of Bidri ware thus lies in the contrast between the shiny inlaid design and the dark matte ground.

Three terms describe the method of metal inlay: *zarnishan*, when the inlaid design is level with the surrounding area; *zarboland*, when the silver inlay rises above the surrounding area; and *aftabi*, when the designs are cut out of a piece of sheet silver so that they appear silhouetted against the body of the vessel.[1]

The compressed spherical vessel is the base of a *huqqa*, an Indian water pipe used for smoking hashish, opium, and tobacco. The *huqqa* consists of several parts: a spherical or bell-shaped base, a detachable tobacco bowl, and a long tube with a mouthpiece through which the cooled smoke is drawn. The pipe gives forth a gurgling sound when used, thus another name for the *huqqa* is the hubble-bubble.

The neck of this *huqqa* base has a standard chevron-inlaid ring and a projecting molding decorated with lotus petals. A wide band of silver inlay in the *zarnishan* method depicts an undulating landscape filled with trees, flowers, and fish-filled ponds as well as birds and animals. The composition includes pavilions full of niches containing vessels of inlaid brass, an architectural element often found in Indian miniature paintings. The decorative zone is bound top and bottom by four more concentric bands of floral motif. While the meaning of the motif is unclear, the design, with its architectural elements, is unique. Bidri ware is usually shown with overall floral or geometric motifs, and vessels with pictorial elements are very rare. This stunning piece of exquisite beauty and superb workmanship has been executed by a master artisan at the highest level of his craft; it must have been commissioned by a discerning patron, possibly as a present for the court.

The Bidri plate is also ornamented in the *zarnishan* method of inlay, using a combination of silver and brass. The lotus medallion in the center is surrounded by seven concentric bands of decorations, both geometric and floral, based on Mughal and Deccani designs. Contrasted against the dark background, the floral motif swirls with rhythmic vitality, and the silver sunburst patterns seem to glow with life. The inlay is done with precision and care, and like the *huqqa* base, it must have been commissioned by people of some means. — T. T. B.

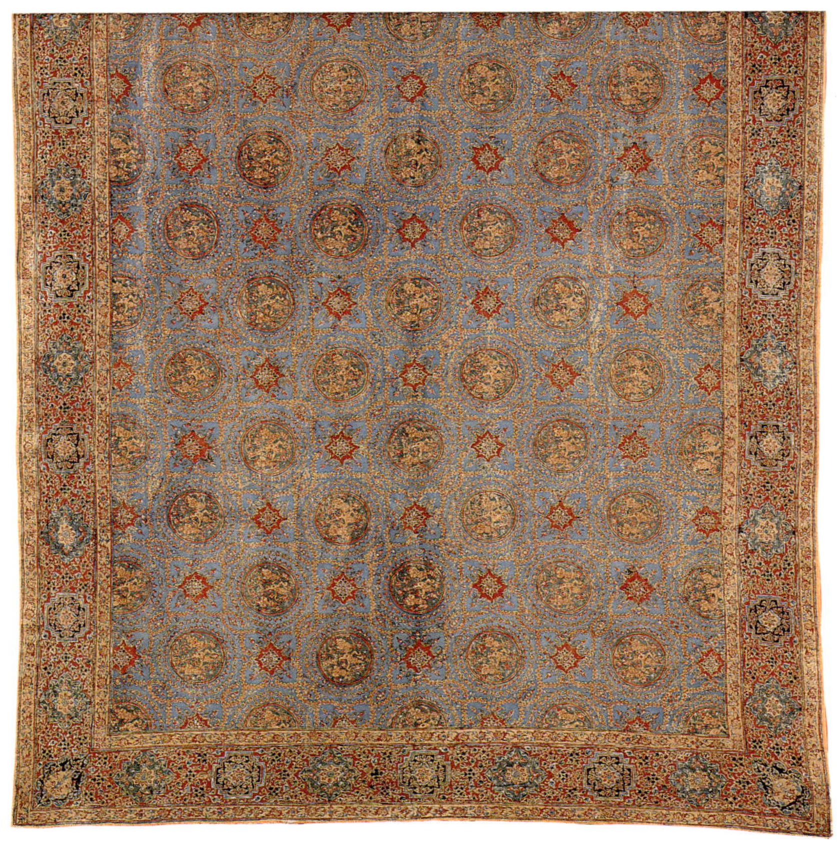

12. PHA KIAO (DETAIL)

India; ca. 1750
Cotton with wax-resist dye
L: 245.1 cm (96½ in.) W: 120.6 cm (47½ in.)
1988.46
Gift of Mr. and Mrs. M. Glenn Vinson, Jr.

Although Indian artisans produced painted and wax-resist decorated cottons as early as the second millennium B.C., it was not until the fifteenth and sixteenth centuries that they expanded their markets to include Europe, Southeast Asia, and the Far East.[1] To do so, they incorporated designs and motifs palatable to the tastes of their foreign patrons. By the seventeenth century, according to one writer, "Everyone from Cape of Good Hope to China, man and woman, is clothed from head to foot" in Indian silks and cottons.[2]

Textiles were so important to Thai commerce that in 1690, the king of Thailand instituted cotton production. The success of this enterprise is not chronicled, but textiles continued to be the country's primary import, a key commodity in the international trade between the Western world, Southeast Asia, and China.

This mid-eighteenth-century *pha kiao* (a textile with four borders) is one of the textiles made specifically for the Thai market. The *pha kiao* may have been used on an elephant or as a room divider, rather than as an article of clothing. The inclusion of figures in the central medallions and the gold applied to the surface indicate that it was made for royalty, as only a royal personage was allowed to use textiles with figural representations and gold. The figures are *thepanom*, adoring figures also found painted and sculpted on Thai architecture and on ceramics produced in China for the Thai market.

The four borders of this *pha kiao* are of equal width and contain alternating octagonal and floral medallions. The border background is red with white wax-resist designs and detailing in green, blue, yellow, and black. Like the border, the central areas were hand-drawn in (white) resist, which was afterward washed out, and then either stamped or hand-drawn with yellow and red mordants. In this instance, the order of the application of dyes seems to be black, red, blue, yellow. (One eighteenth-century source suggests this is the usual order.)

On the basis of technique, this piece can be dated to approximately 1750. Early period works (1720–1750) include white areas of wax resist, while the technique of later pieces degenerated and made less use of this time-consuming method.[3] According to some scholars, the blue background may also indicate an early date. —N.H.

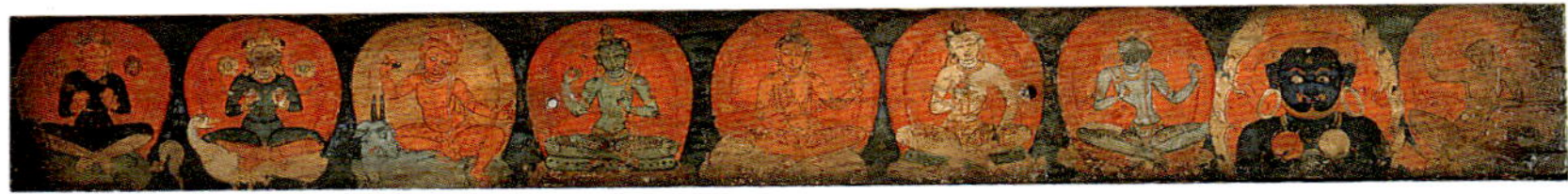

13. BOOK COVER DECORATED WITH THE NINE PLANETARY DEITIES

Nepal; 12th–13th century
Painted wood and gilt copper repoussé
H: 5.7 cm ($2^{1}/_{2}$ in.) L: 46.3 cm ($18^{1}/_{4}$ in.)
1989.2.1
Gift of George Hopper Fitch

In Nepal, books are not bound but resemble Indian texts, which are written on long rectangular pages of birch bark or palm leaf. Paper as well as palm leaf became a popular medium in Nepal as early as the twelfth century.[1] The pages are perforated, placed between wooden slabs, and then strung together by a cord passing through the perforations. These wooden slabs or book covers are often decorated with painted images, the amount of embellishment depending upon the means and taste of the owner.

The owner of this lavishly decorated book cover must have been a man or woman of some means. The top is encased with a sheet of copper repoussé, with a central design of a lotus blossom with two leafy scrolls containing tendrils, blossoms, and buds branching off exuberantly to the two edges, in the ornate curvilinear style typical of Nepalese art. A beaded border surrounds the design. The copper was once gilded; a few small patches of gold remain. The cover is pierced by two holes, so that the cord used for tying the loose manuscript pages can pass through.

The Navagrahas (Nine Planetary Deities) are painted on the reverse. Starting from the right, they are: Aditya (Sun) seated on a horse, holding two lotuses; Chandra (Moon) seated on a swan, also carrying two lotuses; Mangala (Mars) seated on a goat; Budha (Mercury) holding bow and arrow; Brihaspati (Jupiter) holding a book; Sukra (Venus) holding prayer beads and vase; Sani (Saturn) carrying sword and beads and riding on a tortoise; Rahu, who causes eclipses, holding the sun and the moon, and who represents the ascending mode of the moon's orbit; and Ketu, brandishing a sword, the descending mode of the moon's orbit. The gods are each surrounded by a halo shown against a blue background. A small blossom is seen in the blue ground, a characteristic of early Nepalese art. With their elegant proportions the figures reflect the Pala style, but the articulate linear brushwork endowing them with soft, rounded forms is more typically Nepalese.

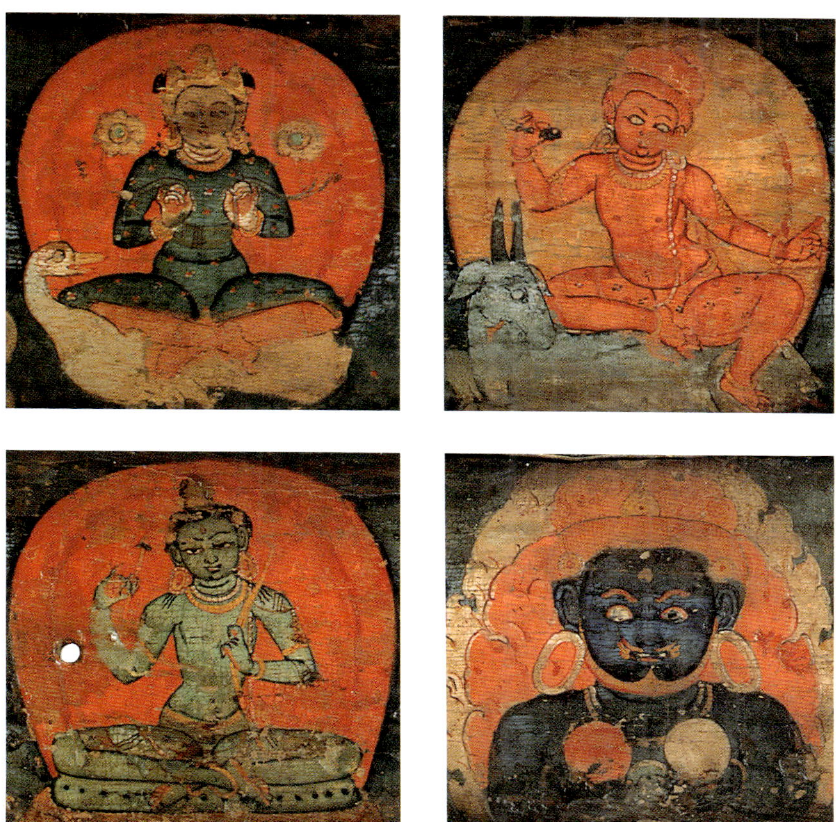

Without the manuscript, it is difficult to ascertain the subject matter. Since the planetary deities enjoyed equal popularity among the Hindus and Buddhists of Nepal, it is not even possible to say whether this book cover once belonged to a Hindu or Buddhist text. The cover is not inscribed, so the identity of the owner is also unknown.

Early Nepalese book covers encased in copper repoussé are very rare. One other known example, a set of covers of a *Prajnaparamita* manuscript, dated 1207, is in the Pritzker collection in Chicago.[2] — T. T. B.

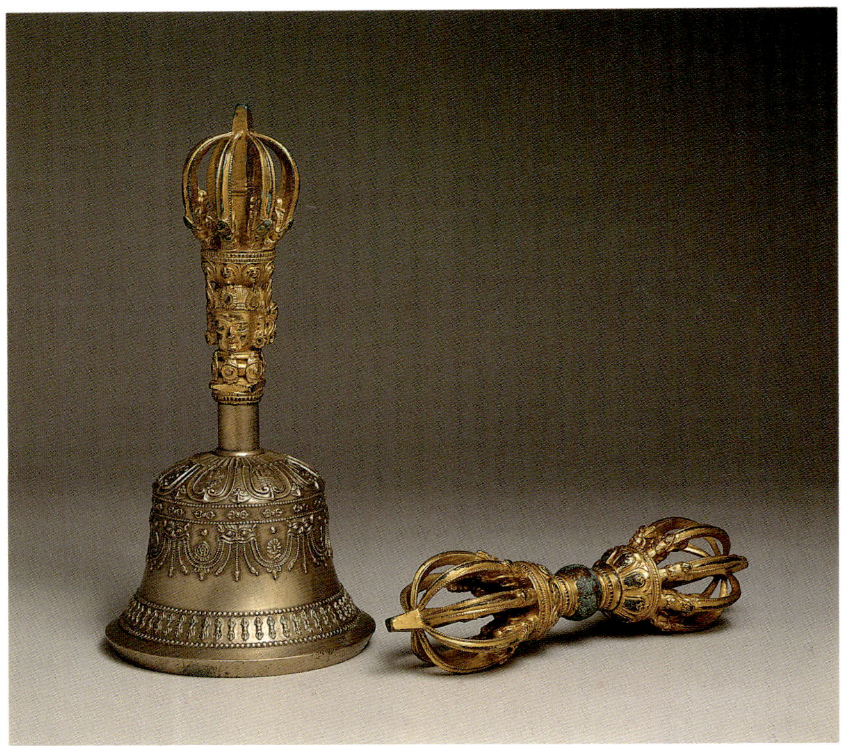

14. THUNDERBOLT AND BELL

Sino-Tibetan; Ming dynasty, Yongle reign (1403–1424)
Gilt metal
Thunderbolt: L: 17.8 cm (7 in.) W: 5.1 cm (2 in.)
Bell: H: 22.9 cm (9 in.) Diam: (at base) 10.8 cm ($4^1/_4$ in.)
85 B3
Gift of Margaret Polak

The Yongle emperor, third emperor of the Ming dynasty, commissioned this superb pair of ritual objects. A fervent Buddhist, the Yongle emperor invited the heads of various Tibetan Buddhist sects to visit China, among them the Fifth Karmapa and head lamas of the Gelug and Sakya sects. These high lamas gave religious instruction to the emperor, and in return, he bestowed titles upon them and gave them fabulous presents, including ingots of gold and silver, bolts of silk, brocade garments, bales of tea, gilded bronze images, and ritual objects.

The thunderbolt and bell (Tibetan: *rdo rje* and *dril bu;* Sanskrit: *vajra* and *ghanta*) are the most important ritual objects of Tibetan Buddhism. They are held in the right and left hands of religious practitioners and are a necessary part of their prayers and rituals. The thunderbolt represents the male aspect of fitness of action or skillful means. The bell stands for wisdom or supreme knowledge, a feminine aspect. Used as a pair in rituals, they symbolize the union of these aspects, which leads ultimately to liberation and enlightenment.

The gilt bronze thunderbolt is the nine-prong type, consisting of eight slender curved prongs springing from *makara* heads (crocodile-like mythical beasts of Indian origin) positioned around a center post. The handle of the bell consists of a vase of plenty supporting the head of Prajna, the personification of supreme knowledge, and half a thunderbolt. The broad face of the goddess, together with the distinct five-leaf crown, is consistent in style with bronze images produced during the Yongle era. A row of characters cast in relief inside the bell reads *Yongle nian shi* (donated in the Yongle reign).

These finely cast ritual objects were treasured by the high lamas of Tibet. Their high regard for them was proven 200 years later, in 1780, when the Qianlong emperor of the Qing dynasty celebrated his seventieth birthday. Among the presents he received from the Panchen and Dalai lamas were two sets of thunderbolts and bells similar in style to this pair made during the Yongle and Xuande eras.[1] — T. T. B.

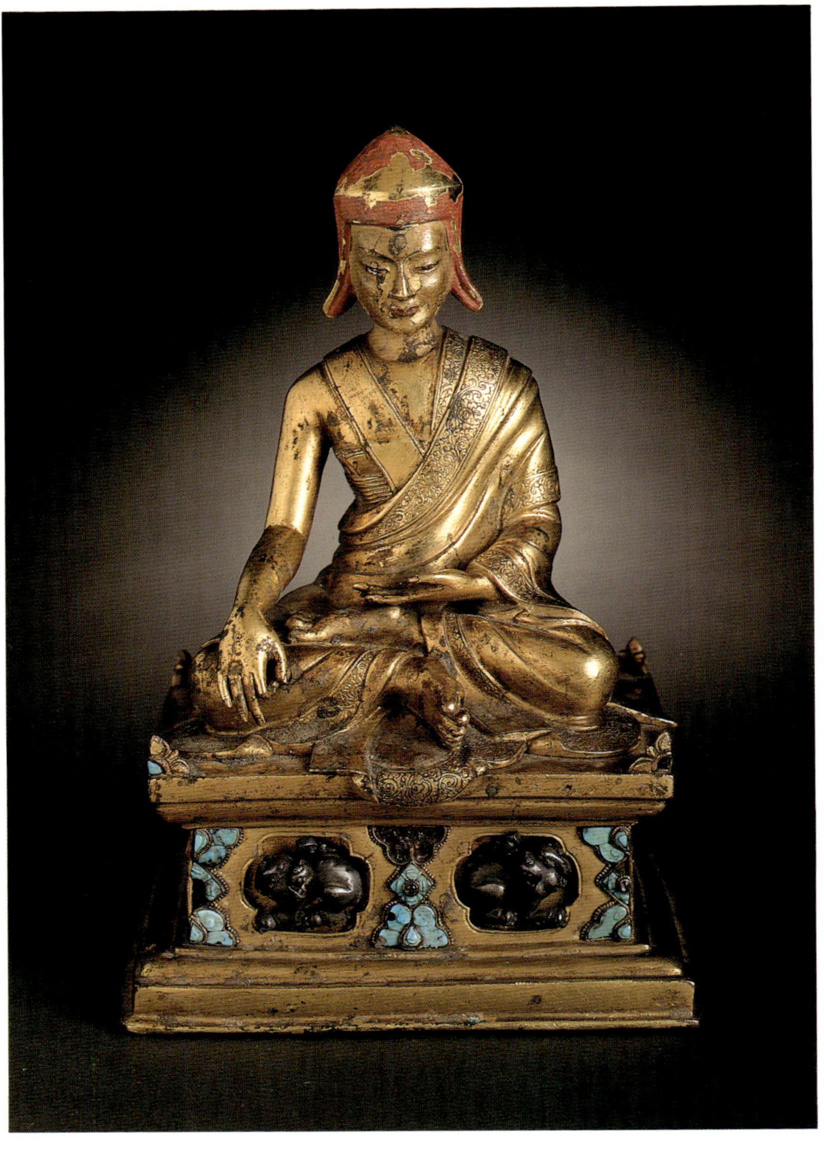

15. IMAGE OF YONGS-'DZIN NGAG-DBANG BZANG-PO

Tibet; ca. 18th century
Gilt bronze inset with turquoise and silver
H: 18.5 cm (7¼ in.) W: 10.5 cm (4⅛ in.)
86 B8
Gift of Raymond G. and Milla L. Handley

The statue is identified by a Tibetan inscription located on the back of the pedestal: Homage to Yongs-'dzin Ngag-dbang bzang-po (pronounced "Yongzin Ngawang zangpo"). Yongs-'dzin Ngag-dbang bzang-po (1546–1615) was an abbot and famous scholar who belonged to the Kagyu sect. He composed the continuation of the autobiography of Padma-dkar-po (Tibetan scholar and historian, 1527–1592).[1]

The lama, wearing a red cap with short lappets, sits in a relaxed pose, his left foot placed above his right. His right hand, palm facing inward, hangs in front of his right knee with first and forefinger touching. His left hand, in the gesture of meditation, has a hole drilled in the middle, indicating that it once held an object. He is in monastic attire; the borders of his garment are finely incised with floral motifs. As is customary with Tibetan images, his face is painted in cold gold (a mixture of gold powder and gelatin that can be brushed on), and his features delineated in colors. His eyes are downcast, and his face bears a serene expression.[2]

The abbot's throne is more elaborate than those usually associated with lamas. Two silver lions with floral motifs set with turquoise and other gems ornament the front, and lotus blossoms, bearing the king's and queen's earrings respectively, appear in quatrefoil openings on the two sides of the throne.

In Tibet it is customary for devotees to commission images or paintings of their teachers, because much importance is placed upon spiritual lineage. An image such as this one could have been commissioned by one of Yongs-'dzin Ngag-dbang bzang-po's students, or by a member of his monastery.
—T. T. B.

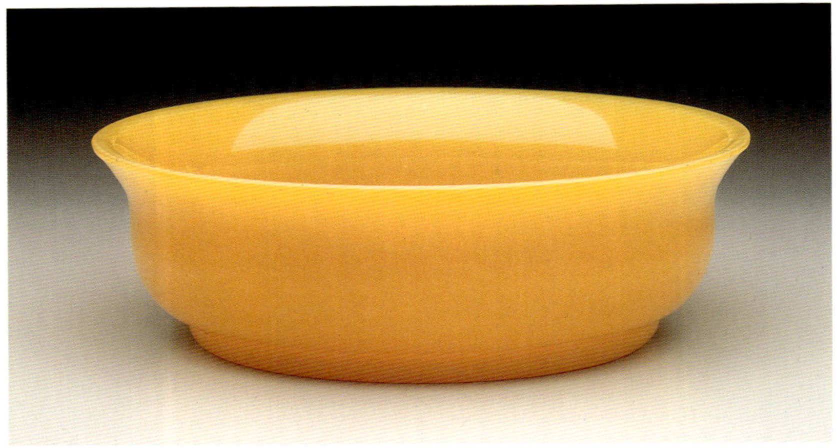

16. TIBETAN BOWL FOR BUTTER-TEA

Sino-Tibetan; probably made at the Boshan factories,
Shandong Province, China, 18th century
Yellow glass, molded and wheel-buffed
H: 4.1 cm (1 5/8 in.) W: 13.3 cm (5 1/4 in.)
1988.44
Gift of Dr. and Mrs. Marvin L. Gordon

Tibetan bowls for butter-tea are distinctively shaped with a broad and shallow cavity, pinched sides for easy cupping in the hands, a slightly splayed mouth rim, and a wide foot ring. Its shallowness facilitates the custom of licking the bowl clean after use. Every Tibetan possesses such a bowl, whether of ordinary wood or, for the more prosperous, of finer wood lined with tin or silver. The wealthy aristocracy, an elite group centered primarily in the Lhasa area, have in addition, for use on special occasions with guests, butter-tea bowls made of high-quality Chinese porcelain, jade, or, rarely, glass. These are usually mounted on a stand and covered with a decorated lid of precious metal, such as silver.

During the second decade of the eighteenth century, the Manchu Yongzheng emperor became a devotee of Tibetan Buddhism. His observance marked the commencement of an era of active relations between Tibet and North China that lasted until the end of the century. Political, tributary, military, cultural, religious, and trade contacts flourished. With Chinese goods more readily available, the Tibetan upper class demanded the finest of objects and materials, including glass, one of the rarer trade items.

During the eighteenth century, Chinese glass for tribute was crafted at the imperial studios in Beijing, and for trade and daily use at commercial studios in Boshanxian, Shandong, and South China's Guangzhou (Canton). The Guangzhou glassmakers favored blown transparent glass; the Boshan factories used fluorite and fluorospar in their glass mix and were more apt to make sturdier opaque and translucent wares. This bowl is attributed to Boshan manufactory, as it bears no imperial-designated mark. Considerable support for this attribution can be found in a historical text by Sun Tingquan, the late seventeenth-century writer and native of Boshan, who was securely knowledgeable about local glassmaking. In his *Yanshan Zaji* (Miscellaneous Notes from Mount Yan), he reports the ingredients for Boshan glass: five parts feldspar, one part fluorite (for opacity), and one part quartz. Small amounts of copper and natural cupritic granules were used to achieve the singular yellow tone.

This bowl has been molded into a specific foreign form with a *bi*-disc-shaped foot ring. The bowl has been polished with a buffing wheel, and any traces of mold leakage and roughness on the rim were ground off before the final buffing, techniques consistent with eighteenth-century glassmaking.

Though wholly Tibetan in origin, the shape of this bowl influenced the making of tea bowls in North China, particularly those made by imperial command. Two were made during the Qianlong era (1735–1795) for the Yonghegong in Beijing, an imperially sanctioned and supported temple. They are porcelain, one with a *faux-bois* (false wood) enameled decoration and the other with a simulated gilt center and *faux-bois* exterior, obviously emulating the common wooden prototypes of Tibet.

Another pair, made of carved lacquer for the Qianlong emperor in 1746 (Avery Brundage Collection, San Francisco), bears verses composed by the emperor and allude to the simple pleasures of tea drinking, to its austerity and purity, and to its ability to evoke spiritual thoughts. —C. F. S.

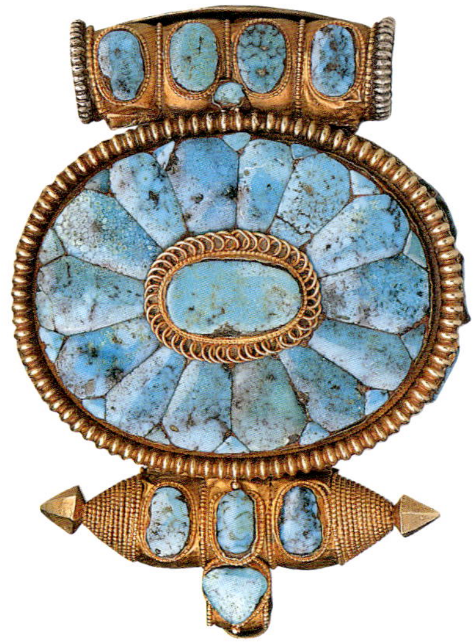

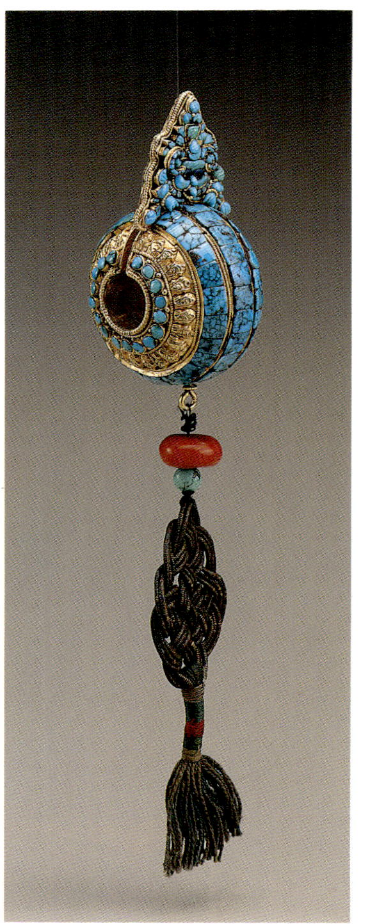

17. GAHU (CHARM BOX)

Tibet; early 20th century, ca. 1930s
Gold, turquoise, and brass
W: 6.3 cm (2½ in.) L: 9.5 cm (3¾ in.)
1988.33
Gift of Margaret Polak

18. CEREMONIAL ORNAMENT

Tibet; 18th–19th century
Gold, turquoise, and lapis lazuli
L: 9.5 cm (3¾ in.) Diam: 6.3 cm (2½ in.)
87 M18
Gift of Margaret Polak

Turquoise (Tibetan: *yu*) is the favorite stone of Tibet. It is worn as beads, set into charm boxes, earrings, and other jewelry, and is also used as a means of exchange in a land where barter is a way of life. Although some turquoise is found in Tibet, a large amount comes from China, Afghanistan, and elsewhere. Tibetans prefer the type of turquoise without flaws or black inclusions, as exemplified by the stones in these two pieces of jewelry. While silver jewelry set with turquoise is plentiful in Tibet, objects of gold are rare. They are usually associated with the nobility and the ruling class.

This golden charm box of superb quality was no doubt the possession of a noblewoman of Lhasa. The shape is traditional, consisting of an oval box with pieces of turquoise set in the shape of a flower. It is a larger version of a *ta-gau*, the hair ornament worn by noblemen of Lhasa.[1] The top tubing encrusted with turquoise is hollow, so that the charm box can be strung and worn around one's neck. The bottom tube has three turquoise pieces and two faceted terminals with gold beading; attached to it is a small loop also set with turquoise. The gold work is extremely fine, and the filigree on the side is typical of the work done in Lhasa in the 1930s.[2] The back piece is of brass and is contoured so as to protect the delicate gold work in front. The charm box is now empty. Small sacred images and rolls of printed prayers and charms are among the objects associated with such boxes, worn traditionally by both men and women of Tibet to ward off evil. Charm boxes for men are larger in size; shrine-shaped boxes to be used while traveling are usually strapped to one's arm.

The ceremonial ornament is a unique object worn by Tibetan nobility on formal occasions, especially during the New Year celebration period. The circular ornament has seven decorative bands separated by gold beading. The three middle bands are inlaid with squares of turquoise, followed by two bands of lotus petals in gold, a motif often seen on silver charm boxes. Surmounting the opening is a *kyung* bird (Sanskrit: Garuda) inlaid with turquoise, ruby, and lapis lazuli. Originally from India, this motif occurs often in Himalayan art and acts as an apotropaic symbol to protect against evil.

This ornament is actually the left half of the gold regalia worn across the shoulder as part of the *gya-lu che* costume (the "garment of royalty," a complex assemblage representing the costume of the ancient Tibetan) worn by officials of Tibet.[3] Spencer Chapman, who went to Lhasa in 1936–1937 as secretary to Mr. B. J. Gould (head of the British Mission to Tibet), described this garment:

> The junior officials wore a most attractive dress called *Geluche*. This consists of a short jacket of very thick brocade with long sleeves made up of several transverse strips of different coloured material.... On each shoulder, set towards the front, were turquoise and gold ornaments, one shaped like a whelk shell and the other a flat rosette. In former times these were suspended from the top of the head and worn as earrings.[4]

This example is obviously the whelk-shell type.[5] Noblemen wearing the *gya-lu che* costume and the ornament similar to this one can be seen in various photographs from old Tibet.[6]—T. T. B.

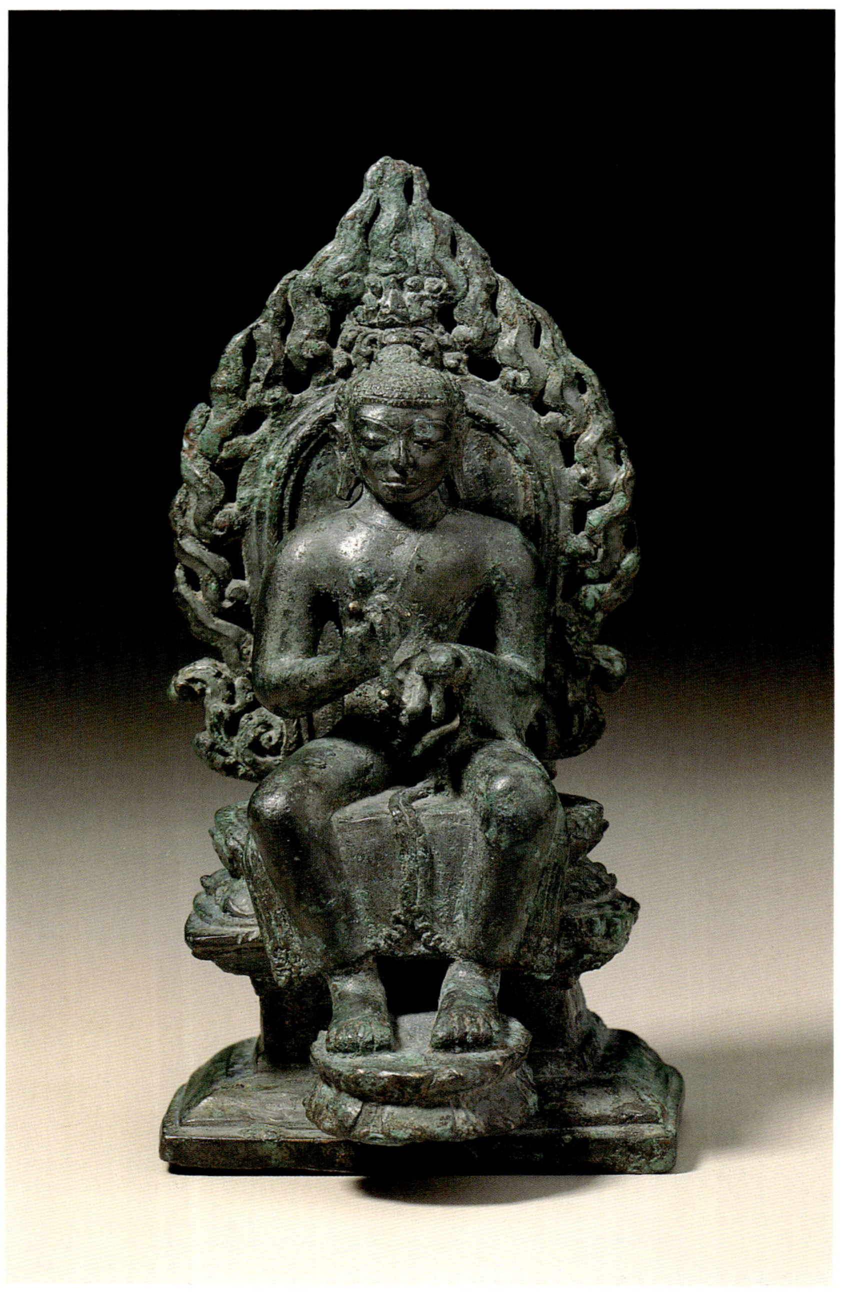

19. BUDDHA

Java, Indonesia; 9th century
Bronze
H: 17.1 cm (6¾ in.) W: 8.6 cm (3⅜ in.)
1988.21
Gift of the LEF Foundation

Small portable bronzes of Buddhist and Hindu figures made their first appearance in Southeast Asia in the fourth century. Stylistically, the earliest bronzes recall South Indian and Sinhalese sculpture; in fact, some of them may well have been manufactured in India. In the fifth and sixth centuries, Southeast Asian artists were inspired by the North Indian Gupta style. In Indonesia, the next major influence was exemplified by the similarity between the Pala-style bronzes of North India and the Central Javanese bronzes of the eighth through tenth centuries. This Buddha falls into that group of sculptures.

The portability of these bronzes makes it difficult to associate them with specific regions, while the lack of inscriptions leaves us with little hope of associating works with patrons.[1] We do know that it was common throughout the Buddhist world for both lay and religious worshipers to commission images. Through the commission of a sculpture, temple, votive tablet, or painting, people acquired religious merit for themselves and their families.

The Buddha is seated with legs in European pose, like the famous image from Candi Mendut (dating to 800) in Central Java.[2] Also like the Mendut sculpture, his hands are in *dharmachakra* mudra. This iconography is common in Central Javanese Buddhas. The bodhisattvas Avalokiteshvara and Vajrapani, accompanying the Candi Mendut Buddha, suggest an identification of this iconographic form of the Buddha as Vairochana—an important figure in ninth-century Javanese Buddhism.

Stylistically, this piece relates to other ninth-century Javanese sculptures. The pleasing proportions of the body, the drapery rippling between the legs, and the treatment of the base and aureole support a ninth-century date.[3] The stippling found on both the throne back and the lotus footrest are reminiscent of this motif on both the clothing and thrones of other Central Javanese bronzes.[4]—N.H.

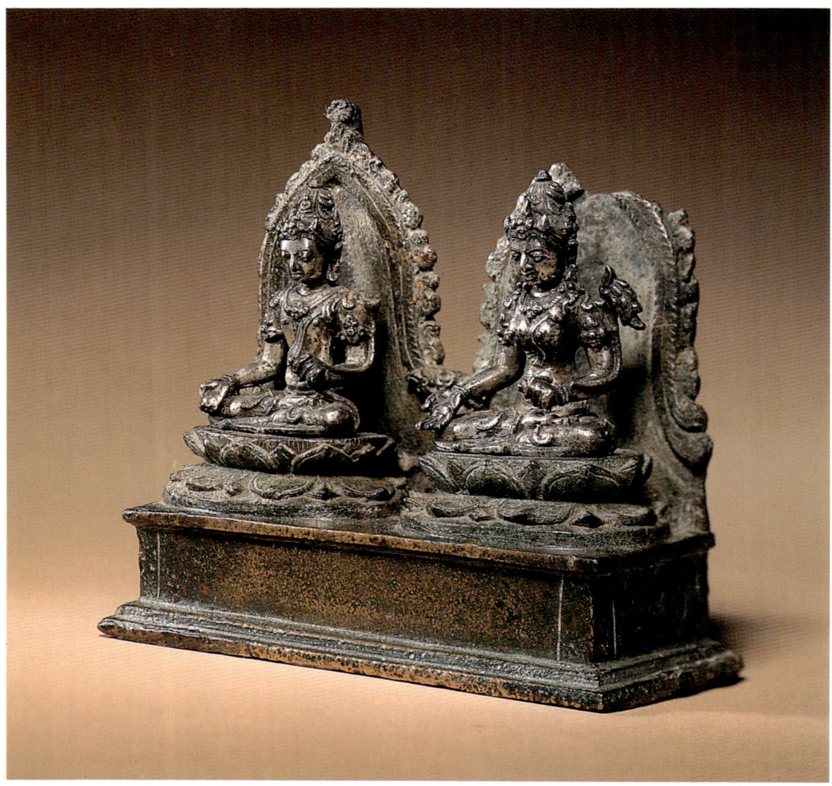

20. AVALOKITESHVARA AND VASUDHARA

Java, Indonesia; 10th–11th century
Silver and bronze
H: 12.1 cm (4¾ in.) L: 13.1 cm (5⅛ in.) W: 5.1 cm (2 in.)
86 B1
Gift of the Walter and Phyllis Shorenstein Fund

The island of Java in the Indonesian archipelago once produced some of the world's finest metal sculpture. From both Buddhist and Hindu traditions, these works served a religious function in temples and personal shrines.

This sculpture of Avalokiteshvara and Vasudhara is an exquisite example of the small personal images produced in Java during the eighth through thirteenth centuries. Both bodhisattvas were important in the Javanese Buddhist pantheon—Avalokiteshvara in his universally appealing role as the compassionate one, and Vasudhara as a fertility figure. Her attribute, a sheaf of rice, helps explain her popularity in the rice-growing regions of Java and northeastern India.

Yet the pairing of these two is unusual and does not relate to any known text, suggesting they may have been added to this pedestal at a later date.

There are numerous examples of silver figures on bronze pedestals in Indonesian art.[1] Because of their stylistic similarity, we can be certain the figures were part of a group of iconographically related figures, possibly representing a mandala.[2]

The production of a group of related images, such as a mandala used for meditational purposes, would have been a costly undertaking, especially with a group of silver images. Thus, we can surmise that a wealthy patron commissioned these silver bodhisattvas.

The figures are seated on separate double lotuses in *virasana* (half-lotus) posture. The male's right hand is in *varada* mudra (gift-bestowing gesture), his left hand holds a lotus, and there is a small Amitabha Buddha in his headdress (identifying him as Avalokiteshvara). The rice stalk in her left hand identifies Vasudhara. Her right hand is in *varada* mudra, while her crown contains a jewel.

On the basis of distribution of sites, Hindu and Buddhist Javanese art is divided temporally into two periods, a Central Javanese period (eighth to early tenth centuries) and an Eastern Javanese period (tenth through sixteenth centuries). Reasons for this regional shift in population and production remain unclear. Dramatic changes in the sculptural and architectural styles from one period to the other reflect an increased interest and reliance on indigenous forms.

These figures lack some of the fleshy roundness that typifies the earlier Central Javanese style, as well as the exaggerated angularity of later Eastern Javanese sculptures. We can date this sculpture on the basis of its figural style; few images from this transitional period have been identified. —N.H.

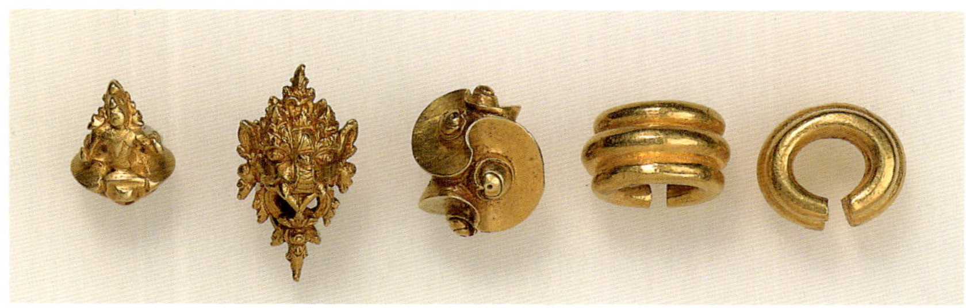

21. GOLD JEWELRY

(left to right)

VISHNU EAR ORNAMENT
Java, Indonesia; 11th–12th century
Gold
H: 1.7 cm (11/16 in.) W: 1.3 cm (1/2 in.)
1988.17
Gift of Francesca M. Bacon

MAKARA EAR ORNAMENT
Java, Indonesia; 13th–14th century
Gold
W: 1.5 cm (9/16 in.) L: 3.0 cm (1 3/16 in.)
1988.19
Gift of Marjorie Bissinger Seller

MEANDERING CLOUD EARRING
Java, Indonesia; 11th–12th century
Gold
H: 1.8 cm (11/16 in.) W: 1.5 cm (9/16 in.)
87 M17
Gift of Mrs. Linda Noe Laine in memory of the Honorable Clare Booth Luce

PAIR OF HAIR ORNAMENTS
Java, Indonesia; 10th–14th century
Gold
H: 1.1 cm (7/16 in.) W: 1.9 cm (3/4 in.)
1988.18a–b
Gift of Marion Greene, an anonymous donor, and the Asian Art Museum General Acquisitions Fund

In modern Indonesia, gold ornament is a symbol of status and power.[1] Gold ornaments are among the most common artifacts from the seventh through sixteenth centuries.

The few gold objects that have been excavated in Java come from temple foundations or graves. Surprisingly, most of the seventh- through sixteenth-century gold recovered from Java has been found in hoards often buried in cylindrical containers of bronze or clay.[2] Accidental finds have been another important source for the recovery of these objects. Because of the lack of archaeological context, the dating of jewelry is still highly conjectural,

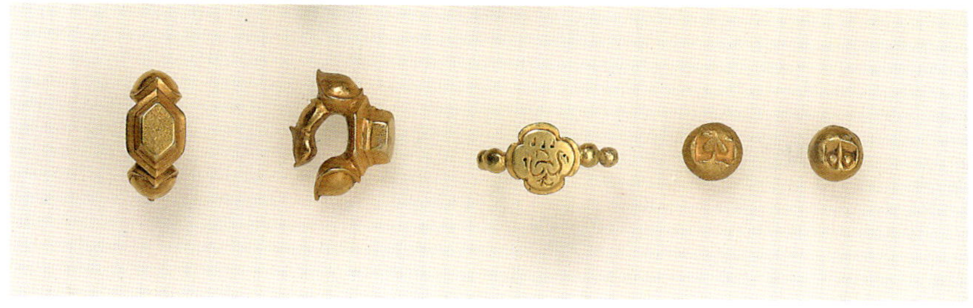

PAIR OF EARCUFFS
Java, Indonesia; 10th century
Gold
W: 1.7 cm (11/16 in.)
1988.15a–b
Gift of Marjorie Bissinger Seller and Marion Greene

RING
Java, Indonesia; 9th–12th century
Gold
Diam: 1.7 cm (5/8 in.)
1988.14
Gift of Mrs. Virginia Lee Taylor

COINS
Java, Indonesia; 14th century
Gold
Diam: 0.6 cm (1/4 in.)
1988.16a–b
Gift of Francesca M. Bacon

although a few objects can be dated by comparison with stone and bronze sculpture.

Early Indian and Chinese sources suggest that Java was rich in gold mines. Javanese inscriptions mention both goldsmiths and gold mines, although we have yet to discover either mines or smithies in Java proper. The ruler Sanjaya refers to this wealth in an inscription dated 732.[3] Gold from this period was worked in a variety of ways.

The most common method of jewelry production in Java during this nine-hundred-year span was casting, rather than the repoussé technique more commonly employed today. Only the hair ornaments (1988.18a–b) in this group were produced differently, by soldering together two smooth tubes of gold; the copper solder gives the gold its slightly pinkish cast. The design is typical of hair ornaments from the tenth through fourteenth centuries.

Rings are the most abundant item of jewelry from this period. Numerous inscriptions mention gold rings given as tribute to temples or royalty.[4] The motif on this delicately cast piece (1988.14) seems to be a symbol of the goddess Sri. One author has shown that the motif evolved from the word *Sri* written in old Javanese script on the earliest rings.[5] Rings with this motif have been discovered throughout Southeast Asia, in contexts suggesting a seventh- through tenth-century date.

Ear ornaments are numerous and diverse, ranging from the small, geometrically designed earcuffs (1988.15a–b)[6] and Vishnu ornament (1988.17)[7] to the more elaborately cast *makara* (1988.19)[8] and meandering cloud ornaments (87 M17).[9] Earcuffs were worn on the upper part of an extremely elongated earlobe, as we see in numerous examples of stone sculpture from the earliest period of Central Javanese art through the Eastern Javanese period.[10] The smallest examples, like the Vishnu ear ornament, may have been used to decorate bronze or stone sculptures.[11] This Vishnu can be identified by the stylized Garuda upon which he sits.

The clearly defined, three-dimensional meandering cloud decoration on the largest earcuff dates it; such cloud motifs were prominent in the relief sculpture of the eleventh and twelfth centuries in Central and South Central Java. (The eleventh-century site of Selamangleng on Tulung Agung is a notable example.) In Bali, the clouds framing the relief sculpture of the site of Yeh Pulu, near Bedulu, provide an even better comparison.[12]

The *makara*, a South and Southeast Asian crocodilian, was a popular motif in architecture and sculpture, as well as on jewelry. Here, the larger front part of the earring depicts an elephant-snouted *makara* rearing his head out of profuse foliage. The smaller side of the earring is more abstract, an extension of the foliage from which the *makara* emerges. The detail of the earring is extremely fine, reminiscent of the detail of the jewels worn by sculptural figures of the ninth through fourteenth centuries.

Piloncito coins (1988.16a–b) of both silver and gold were common currency in Southeast Asia. These examples, one decorated with a tree motif and the other with two small dots, are typical of coins found at sites of the Majapahit period. Chinese coins replaced Javanese currency in 1350.[13]—N.H.

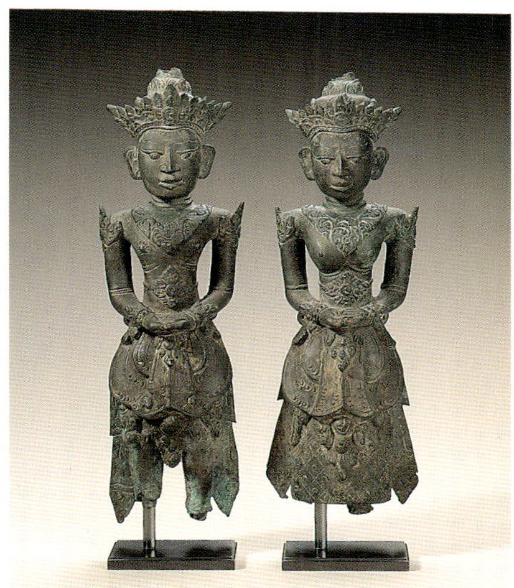

22. FUNERARY FIGURES

Bali, Indonesia; 15th–16th century
Bronze
H: (*a*) 36.0 cm (14 1/8 in.),
(*b*) 37.9 cm (14 7/8 in.)
W: (both figures) 11.3 cm (4 1/2 in.)
86 B6a–b
Gift of the Connoisseur's Council, Shawn and Brook Byers, and the Asian Art Museum General Acquisitions Fund

These rare bronze figures, like the stone Javanese female (cat. no. 23), probably were funerary sculptures. The syncretic Balinese religion assimilates Hindu-Buddhist beliefs and an indigenous religion in which ancestor worship plays a prominent role. The use of bronze for an image is unusual in Bali; wood or other perishable materials are the traditional media.

In the period preceding the creation of these pieces, a strongly Hindu-oriented Javanese influence was responsible for the creation of a large number of stone sculptures. This bronze couple echoes many stylistic features of the stone images' pose, clothing, crown type, and jewelry, suggesting that the stone and bronze figures were used for the same purpose.[1] Inscriptional evidence suggests the stone works were commissioned by individuals.[2]

Both male and female figures stand in a rigid frontal pose, hands crossed in a manner suggesting they may have once held an offering. Their clothing, jewelry, and crowns are practically identical, indicating they are a pair commissioned by the descendants of the deceased to accept the soul during specified rituals.

Present Balinese practice requires a cremation long after the death and burial of an individual. Often a few families share the costs of offerings. Sometimes years after the death, purification of the soul takes place, a ritual requiring effigies representing both the body and the soul.

The strong magical quality ascribed to metal would have made these bronzes particularly powerful and important images.[3] A group of comparable pieces were considered so sacred they were kept hidden in a temple until an attempted theft first brought them to light in 1928.[4]

Bronze works of this style have previously been dated to the fourteenth century, but the radiocarbon dating of these two sculptures places them between the fifteenth and sixteenth centuries. —N.H.

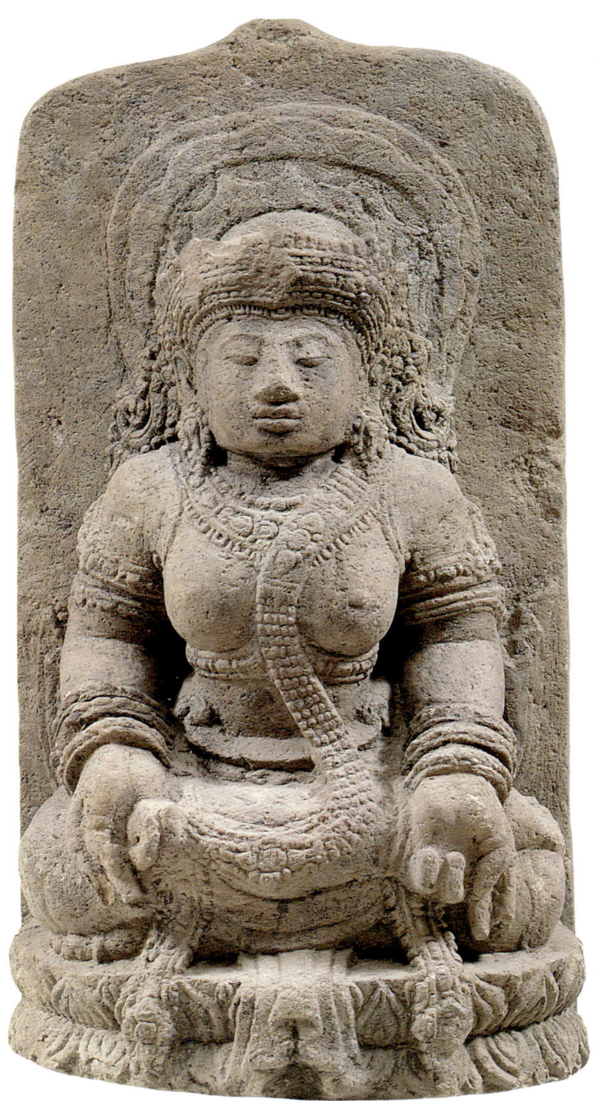

23. FEMALE SCULPTURE

Java, Indonesia; Kediri, 13th–14th century
Tufa
H: 53.3 cm (21 in.) W: 28.6 cm (11¼ in.)
87 S6
Gift of Marion Greene

From the seventh to the fifteenth century, India's Hindu and Buddhist belief systems strongly influenced the peoples of Java. The seventh through tenth centuries marked the political importance of Central Java, where temples similar in conception to Indian temples were constructed to honor Buddha, Shiva, and Vishnu. In the eleventh century, the political center shifted to East Java, and temples of a more distinctly Javanese style and decoration appeared. The assertion of Javanese style coincides with the resurgence of indigenous religions, which combined with Hinduism and Buddhism to form a single syncretic religion.

In the indigenous religions of Indonesia, ancestors are often considered bridges between gods and men. This seated female may have been intended as a funerary sculpture, carved as a seat for the soul of the deceased.

Images like this Kediri piece are found in both Java and Bali.[1] The iconography of the figures, usually standing, varies and often does not allow for a Buddhist or Hindu interpretation of the sculpture—possible proof of their role as ancestor figures. Some of the frequently shared characteristics of these sculptures may include a round object held in one or both hands and a pleated pattern circling the figure or its head.

A recent anthropological study of the Tengger peoples of Eastern Java assists our understanding of the religious practices of twelfth- through fifteenth-century eastern Javanese and Balinese peoples.[2] The Tengger, although politically and economically close to the modern Javanese,[3] practice a religion based on Hindu-Buddhist thought, one closely related to the present Balinese religion. Part of its ritual involves the use of flower images that, it is believed, provide a locus or seat for the souls of their dead ancestors. This sculpture may have served the same function in thirteenth- and fourteenth-century Java.

The sculpture is elaborately decorated with earrings, crown, necklaces, bracelets, and armbands. The jewels of her crown, entwined with her hair, fall in an elaborate cascade over her shoulders. She sits with legs crossed, and her two hands rest on her knees. The palm of the left hand faces outward and points to the ground. The right hand holds a small round object, possibly a clod of earth alluding to her function as a funerary image. —N.H.

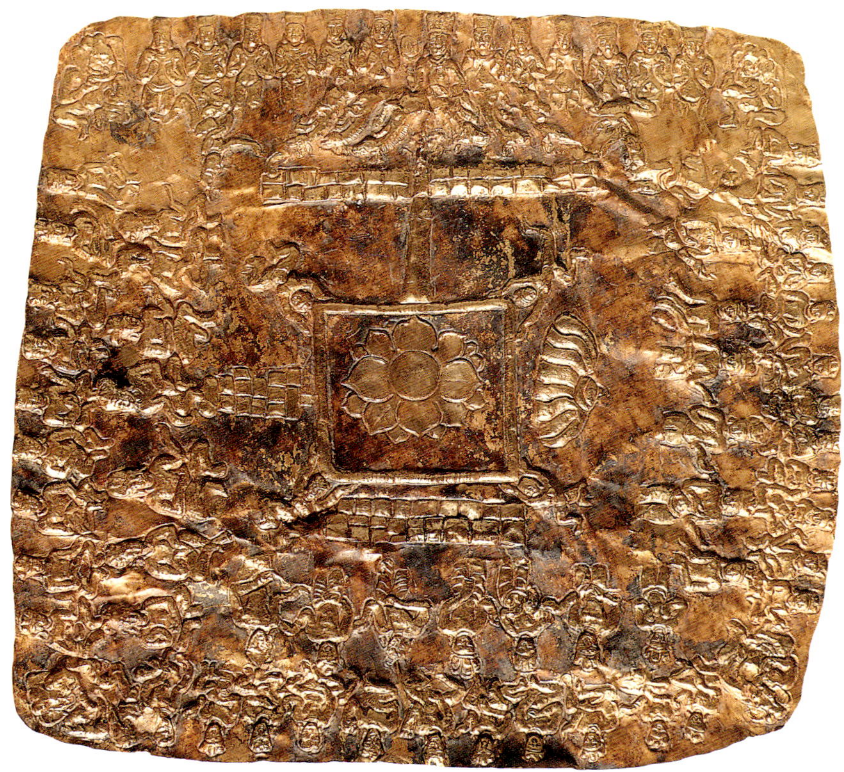

24. DEDICATORY PLAQUE

Southeast Asia; 8th–9th century
Gold repoussé
H: 26.7 cm (10½ in.) W: 29.2 cm (11½ in.)
1988.12
Gift of the Walter and Phyllis Shorenstein Fund

The dedication of a temple in ancient Southeast Asia was both an important religious event and a significant secular occasion. The temple, usually located on a hill, represented a microcosm of the universe—it was the world mountain, the *axis mundi*, a representation of the gods' domain on earth. A ruler legitimized his power through the temple's establishment, and it served as the center of his kingdom.

Gold repoussé images of gods, lotuses, and animals often were buried to commemorate the foundation of a temple. This repoussé dedicatory plaque, much larger and of greater iconographic complexity than any previously discovered, appears to have served this purpose.

The *Agni Purana* states that a tortoise and five objects of cosmological significance should be buried in the foundation of a temple. A cosmological interpretation may also underlie the meaning of this plaque. It is not unusual to find rows of undifferentiated figures, representing the seven classes of beings, depicted in the early Hindu art of India.[1]

The undifferentiated condition of the figures of this plaque make specific identification of all but a few of them difficult. (Like the Indian examples, some of them may represent classes of beings rather than individuals.) A figure of the Hindu god of fortune, Ganesha, appears at each of the four corners. The *adityas* (sun gods) are at the top of the plaque, with a composite Vishnu-Surya image in the center holding the reins of Surya's chariot. This composite figure is unusual, but Puranic literature and a syncretistic tendency in Southeast Asian religion[2] support a syncretic interpretation of it: "He [the Sun] is the very same glorious Lord Narayana [Vishnu], the First Person [the Prime Cause of the universe]."[3]

Below this row of figures and to the right of the central lotus is a single dancing figure who may well represent a personification of Vishnu's *chakra* or discus; the dancing *chakrapurusha* (wheel person) is found only in Northeastern India.[4] The *chakra* plays a particularly important role in Dvaravati-period Buddhist sculpture in Thailand and may illuminate its prominence in this situation. In this instance, Vishnu's *chakra* and the single wheel of Surya's chariot[5] are another aspect of the syncretic nature of the imagery of this large and rare repoussé plaque. Additional research and future archaeological finds may further elucidate its complex iconography. —N.H.

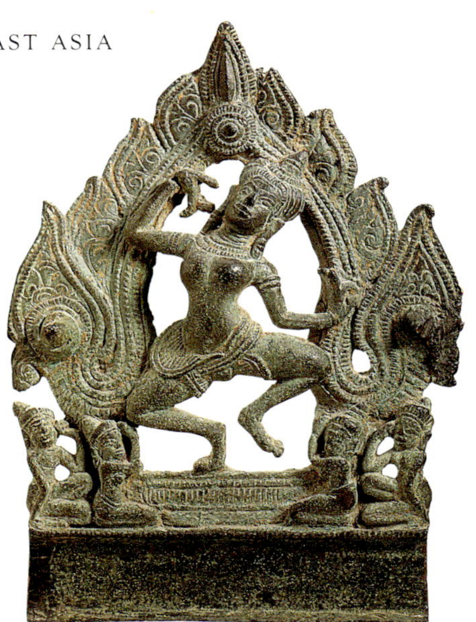

25. APSARA

Cambodia (Kampuchea); 12th–13th century
Bronze
H: 13.7 cm (5 3/8 in.) W: 10.1 cm (4 in.)
83 B2
Gift of Mr. and Mrs. John B. Bunker

This elegant, bronze dancing *apsara* (a heavenly being) undoubtedly served an apotropaic purpose; like auspicious figures sculpted as architectural ornamentation on temples, she is intended to ward off evil. She is accompanied by minor figures wearing the headdress typical of the Angkor Wat style. However, her simple hairdo and heavily wrapped skirt may reflect a slightly later date.

The ornament would have adorned a bronze throne or some other religious paraphernalia, but it is impossible to divine whether it was exalting a Buddhist or Hindu deity, as auspicious beauties adorned bronze objects of both religions.[1] In either case, an individual donor may well have commissioned the piece for his private shrine.

Images of dancing females were a popular subject for sculptors throughout Southeast Asia. No one has been able to satisfactorily identify the dances performed by these females, although they may relate to dances still performed in the region.

In India, specific types of fertility goddesses traditionally decorated Buddhist and Hindu temples. The Khmer also used female imagery to adorn their religious monuments, but these figures do not reflect the Sanskrit descriptions of a fertile woman; rather, they depict the Southeast Asian ideal.

The elemental composition of this piece has been tested, and it has been determined to be of a similar provenance and date as comparably dated bronzes. —N.H.

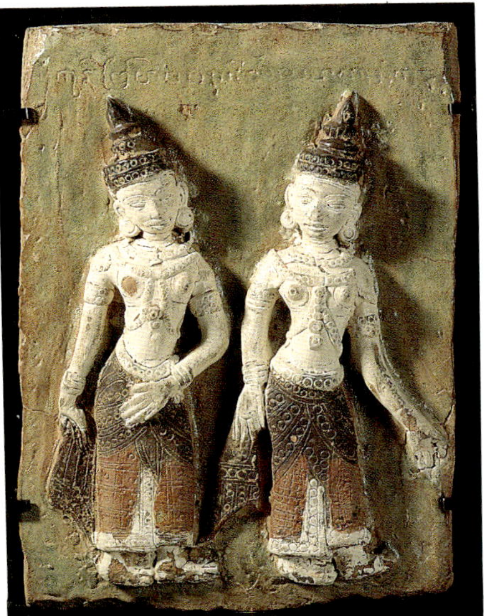

26. THE DAUGHTERS OF MARA

Pegu, Burma; 15th–16th century
Terra-cotta tile
H: 44.0 cm (17½ in.) W: 33.0 cm (13 in.)
86 P14
Purchase: Asian Art Museum General Acquisitions Fund

This terra-cotta tile depicting two jeweled and crowned daughters of Mara would have adorned the exterior of a stupa or temple. Found frequently on Burmese Buddhist monuments, such decorative tiles included scenes either from the life of the Buddha or from the *jatakas* (previous lives of the Buddha).

The accompanying Mon inscription identifies the scene: "Mara's daughter assumes the form of a virgin having no children."[1] This alludes to an episode in the Buddha's life when the demon Mara sent his beautiful daughters as a temptation to obstruct the Buddha's attainment of enlightenment.

Comparable examples are found at the Shwegugyi pagoda near Pegu, which was constructed by King Dhammaceti (r. 1472–1492).[2] The monuments at this site commemorate the seven weeks of the Buddha's search for enlightenment in Bodh Gaya; an unusual architectural iconography reflects the personal choice of the king and his advisers.[3]

The use of terra-cotta plaques dates from the earlier Pagan period of Burmese art. These earlier works tend to have more spatially developed scenery with smaller figures. In fifteenth- and sixteenth-century works, large figures were placed on a blank ground.

In this example, although the figures are frontally posed, the placement of their feet and the draperies that trail behind them create the illusion that they are walking to the right. The glazes are common to tiles of all periods.
—N.H.

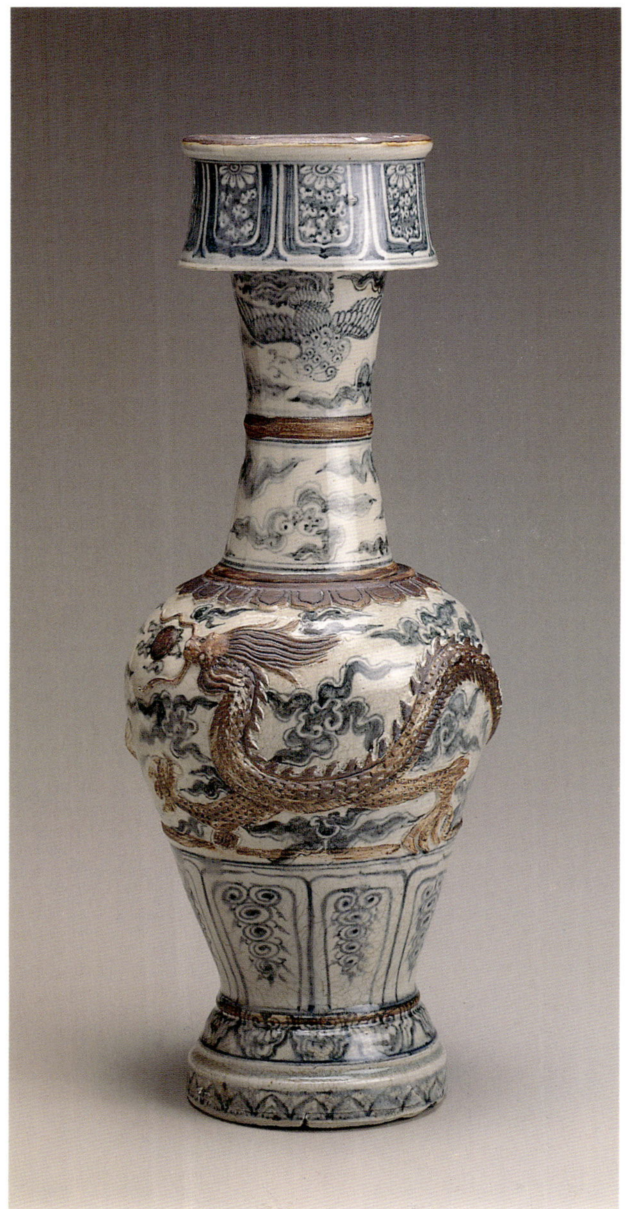

27. TEMPLE VASE

Hai-Ninh Province, Vietnam; Le dynasty,
late 16th–early 17th century
Iron-oxide and cobalt decorated, slipped,
and overglazed stoneware
H: 50.1 cm (19¾ in.) W: 15.2 cm (6 in.)
1988.43
Gift of the Connoisseur's Council

During the late sixteenth and throughout the seventeenth century, the northern regions of present-day Vietnam were plagued by sporadic civil strife. A few overlords and their clans controlled vast territories and were only nominally loyal to the throne of the Le dynasty (1533–1788) in Hanoi, the capital then known as Thanglong (Ascendant Dragon). Two clans in particular, the Trinh and the Nguyen, amassed powerful armies that threatened the whole of Vietnamese society.

As often occurs in times of social unrest and uncertainty, the people sought refuge in religion, resulting in a popular revival of Buddhism and the proliferation of temple construction and patronage. Local gentry supported these temples as a means of accumulating religious merit in order to be reborn into a more peaceful world. Among the objects commissioned were those used on altars for religious practices.

This particular temple vase with candlestick cover was designed so that each could be used independently. As a single composite piece, it may appear somewhat unbalanced to the Western eye, but such construction was a frequent fashion among Annamese temple wares of the sixteenth and seventeenth centuries.[1]

Although crude compared to contemporaneous Chinese Jingdezhen porcelains, the salient features of the vase are totally consistent with traditional Annamese Bat Trang aesthetics and should be evaluated on their own merits. The dominant motif is a four-clawed dragon pursuing a flaming pearl modeled, applied, and slipped in iron oxide, resulting in a matte, unglazed appearance. This Vietnamese hallmark contrasts with the textural surface sheen of the transparent glaze over the cobalt-blue decoration of *ruyi* lappets, false gadroons, and cloud scrolls. The brushwork of these decorative elements is uneven but vigorous, swift, and confident, traits characteristic of the painter-potters of Annam.

The dragon motif, although popular on Chinese porcelains (to which this Vietnamese specimen owes an obvious debt) is rarely found on Vietnamese porcelains other than temple vases. The peacocklike phoenix high on the neck of the vase is strikingly poised and elegant in flight, as it is frequently represented in Annamese blue-and-white ceramics. Yet the uppermost band of floral petals containing scattered flowers is simply a decorative formula derived from early fifteenth-century blue-and-white ware from Jingdezhen, China. Because the fifteenth century had been a time of noted Ming influence in northern Vietnam, the gentry and their Bat Trang potters would undoubtedly have been conversant with the older Ming styles.

The dullish gray tonality of the blue color is due to the potter's use of impure cobalt containing a high percentage of manganese oxide, a characteristic of cobalt from Yunnan Province in Southwestern China. It was more convenient to obtain and cheaper than the purer Persian cobalt, which partially explains the nearly spontaneous appearance of blue-and-white ware in early fifteenth-century Vietnam and the rapid development and expansion of production throughout the end of the seventeenth century. —C.F.S.

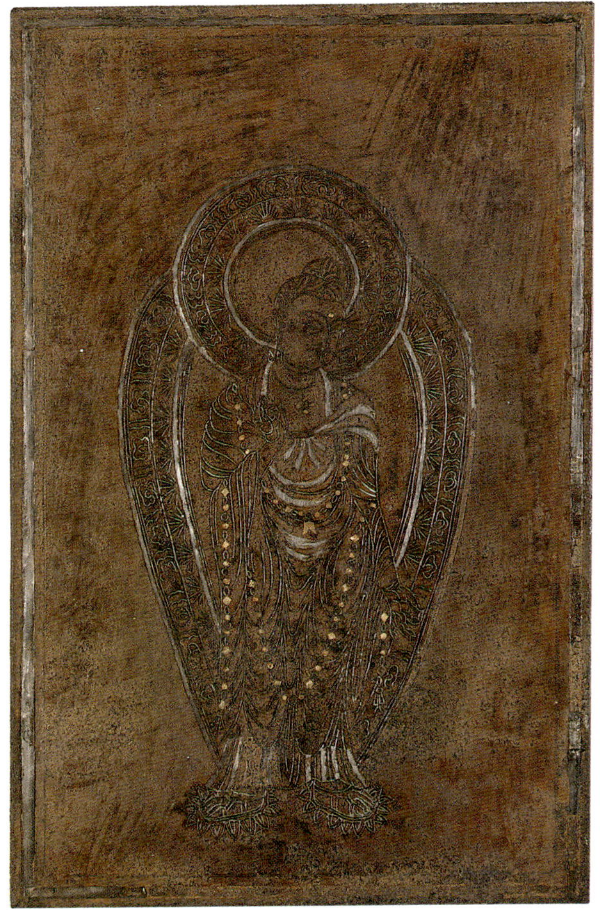

28. JEWELED BUDDHA

Central Asia; Uighur Kingdom of Qocho,
ca. 10th–11th century
Iron plaque inlaid with gold and silver
H: 28.2 cm (11 1/8 in.) W: 17.7 cm (7 in.)
87 B3
Gift of the Connoisseur's Council

As China's control over its frontiers weakened in the last years of the Tang dynasty, a Turkic group called the Uighurs arose along the Silk Road that crosses the Gansu corridor and the northern edge of the Tarim basin. Their most avid desire was to maintain friendly relations with China; they offered tribute of horses and jade in return for the Chinese silk that became the mainstay of their trade with the West. By the tenth century, the Uighurs had established three separate kingdoms, two in present-day Gansu and one, the largest, called Qocho, near modern Turfan, in Xinjiang Province. By that time as well, their rulers, originally converts to Iranian Manichaeism, had converted again, this time to Buddhism. The Uighurs at Qocho supported important Buddhist monasteries within their capital and at the nearby desert sites of Bezeklik and Sangim-aghiz, famous for their impressive fresco cycles.[1]

This iron plaque, inlaid with thin lines of gold and silver, depicts a standing Buddha with a striking resemblance to images in the frescoes of the cave temples of Bezeklik. There, as here, the Buddha is shown in nearly three-quarters view, wearing heavy monastic robes that cover both shoulders, and long strands of jewels around his neck. His right hand is raised in the *vitarka* (discussion) mudra. His heavy form recalls the Tang Chinese preference for sensual bulk, but his thin, curled mustache is distinctly Central Asian, harking back to the art of Gandhara and Kucha. At Bezeklik, similar images form part of elaborate *prahnidhi* (procession) scenes in most of the tenth-century cave temples. Along both walls of each cave, larger-than-lifesize Buddhas proceed toward a central stupa-pillar, the main object of reverence in the temple.

Votive plaques of wood painted with similar images of the Buddha have been found in great abundance at Buddhist sites along the southern Silk Road, such as Dandan-oilik.[2] This example in iron is unique, although at least one other iron object obtained near Lhasa, a corn measure inlaid with a gold and silver Nestorian cross, also has a tenuous connection with Turfan,[3] since tenth-century Turfan was a center of Nestorian Christianity. A cache of the sect's documents was unearthed there in the early twentieth century. Turfan was long the object of Tibetan desires, because of its position of control on the northern Silk Road. Tibet, in fact, held the Turfan region and much of the rest of Turkestan during the eighth century. The Tibetan empire was subsequently smashed, but the Uighur kingdoms of Gansu were taken by a reconstituted Eastern Tibetan kingdom in the early eleventh century.[4]—P. B.

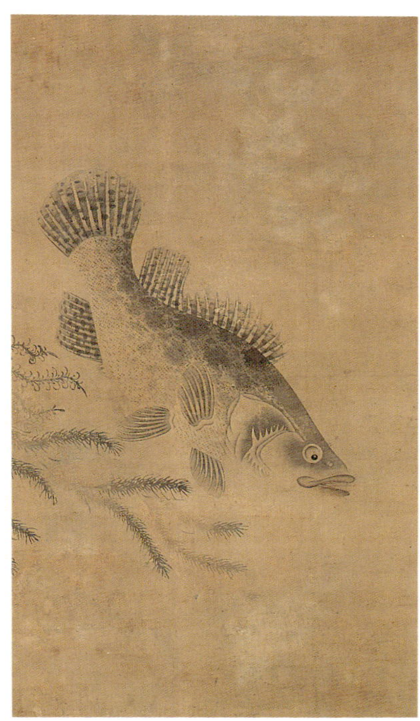
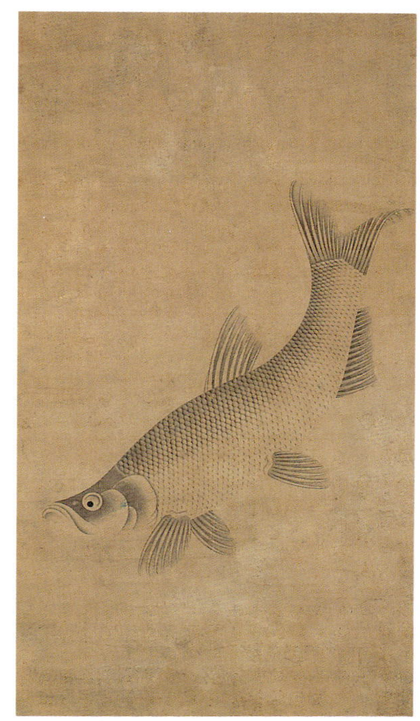

29. TWO FISH AND WATERWEEDS

By Lai'an (ca. late 13th–early 14th century)
China; Yuan dynasty, 1279–1368
Pair of hanging scrolls, ink on paper
H: (*1*) 99.5 cm (39 3/16 in.), (2) 99.0 cm (39 in.)
W: 54.0 cm (21 1/4 in.)
87 D9.1–2
Gift of the Tang Foundation

The iconoclasm of Chan (Zen) Buddhist thinking declared the pantheon of Buddhas and bodhisattvas irrelevant to regular religious practice. Chan Buddhists encouraged adherents to hack up and burn images of the Buddha, indeed, to "kill the Buddha" if they met him on the road. Such strong statements were consistent with their belief that any attachment, material or emotional, stood in the way of enlightenment. But the absorption of Chan Buddhists with ordinary things enabled them to find new models for enlightenment in the natural world. By the Song dynasty, paintings of fish, cranes, and gibbons came to replace or accompany other, more orthodox images in Chan halls. The combination of more standard Buddhist icons with animals, as in the famous Daitokuji triptych of the Chinese monk-painter Muqi's *White-Robed Guanyin, Gibbons*, and *Crane*, was especially popular in Japan. The animals' lack of guile, their ability to move through water, air, or from limb to limb as though free of gravity, their accuracy, quickness, and lack of reflection, made them admirable ideals. These two opposed fish paintings probably served such a symbolic purpose, substituting for the bodhisattvas or other guardian images that flank a central icon as an aid to meditation.

Lai'an was a Yuan-dynasty painter, but he is only recorded in one early sixteenth-century Japanese compilation of Chinese painting, *Kundaikan Sayuchoki*. This catalogue of the collection of Ashikaga Yoshimasa is not an inventory of paintings, but rather ranks the painters of works brought back to Japan by monks returning from their studies in Chinese monasteries. More than half of these artists, like Lai'an, were active during the Yuan period; about one quarter, also like Lai'an, do not appear in any standard Chinese biographical sources.

Lai'an, like many of his contemporaries, may have been a Buddhist priest, which accounts for the relative rarity of his works—only twelve (excluding these two) are associated with his name, some justifiably, some not.[1] Nine of this dozen are attributions only; of the remaining three, none are signed, but all are impressed with his seal, *Lai'an*. All three of these seals are probably later Japanese interpolations; in fact, two actually read *Na'an*. Each of the present scrolls, however, has a clear impression of a seal that reads *Lai'an*. The impressions are old and appear to be contemporary with the painting.

This pair of fish fits well into the stylistic tradition of fish painting that flourished from the Song dynasty on, formulated by such masters as Fan Anren and Liu Cai. This tradition emphasized careful delineation of the scales of the fish using subtle washes of ink, while at the same time creating an effortless sense of life and flexible, weightless movement. —P. B.

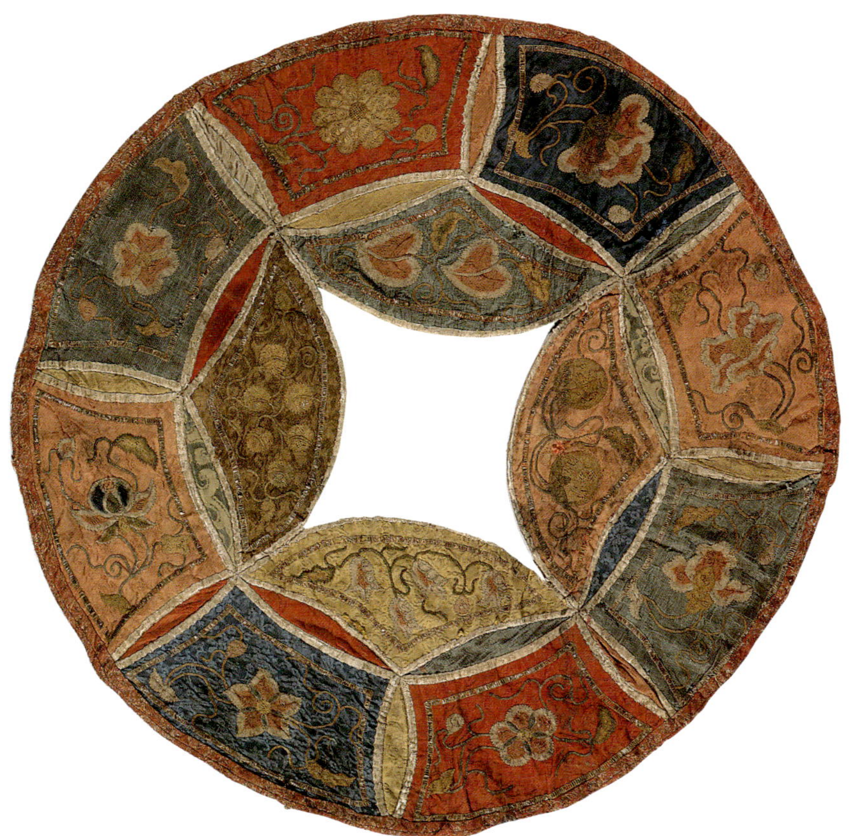

30. MONEY-SHAPED RELIC WRAPPER

China; late Southern Song–early Ming dynasty,
13th–14th century
Patchwork silk embroidered in needle-looping
over gilt paper
Diam: 52.1 cm (20½ in.)
1988.49
Purchase: City Art Trust Fund

Buddhist relics were traditionally handled with an exquisite sense of reverence, which demanded that they be fitted into nested containers, each wrapped with finely worked silks. Some relic wrappers were simple squares of fabric; others, like this money-shaped piece, are elaborately designed auspicious symbols.

Chinese Buddhist devotees often placed money with relics to symbolize good fortune. A reliquary was found buried in an underground chamber at the eleventh-century Xingshengjiao (Doctrine of Prevailing Holiness) temple pagoda in Shanghai, its lid scattered with Song and Tang dynasty coins. Inside it, an image of the Buddha's parinirvana lay on a bed of coins.[1] At the almost contemporary Huqiu (Tiger Mound) pagoda in nearby Suzhou, a nested set of iron reliquary boxes, discovered in the floor of the third story, contained a small shrine wrapped in a money-shaped patchwork of silks.[2]

This money-shaped piece was probably made two or three centuries later, in the last years of the Song dynasty or during the brief Yuan dynasty, when the descendants of the Mongol conqueror Genghis Khan ruled China. The patterns of the fourteen different silks that comprise it—plain weaves, damasks, cords, and brocades—were all woven during the late thirteenth and fourteenth centuries, when China's silk industry burgeoned through increased trade along a unified Silk Road, and when important innovations in drawloom construction allowed weavers greater flexibility in fabric design.

The rare type of needlework that decorates the patchwork of silks, called needle-looping, can also be dated with some precision. Until recently, needle-looping was known only from a few examples preserved in Japan and dating to the thirteenth through sixteenth centuries. One, a small piece with needle-looped flowers now worked into a cushion, belonged to the Chinese Chan priest Wuxue Zuyuan (Mugaku Sogen), founder of Engakuji in Kamakura, Japan, and was carefully preserved by his followers at Nanzenji. The details of Sogen's life are well known.[3] He was born in the last years of the Southern Song dynasty, sometime in the thirteenth century, and studied in the temples dotting the mountains near Hangzhou, then a center of Buddhist studies. He spent much of his life on missions in Southeast Asia and the Ryūkyūs. His fame as a missionary spread, and in 1279, on the eve of the Mongol conquest of South China, he was invited to Japan by the regent Tokimune. He may well have received this piece of needle-looping as a farewell gift from his Chinese disciples.

The needle-looped decoration on this relic wrapper represents the flowers of the four seasons: chrysanthemum, peony, lotus, and plum. Each flower is worked in rows of spiraling loops to produce a knotted, openwork fabric resembling crochet that is attached to the background only at the edges. This technique allowed the artist to back each flower with carefully cut pieces of gilt and silvered paper, which shine subtly through the petals. The twining stems, creating a pattern akin to the blue-and-white floral ceramics of the late Yuan and early Ming, are done in an analogous technique, a square chain stitch also laid over thin strips of gilt and silvered paper. —P. B.

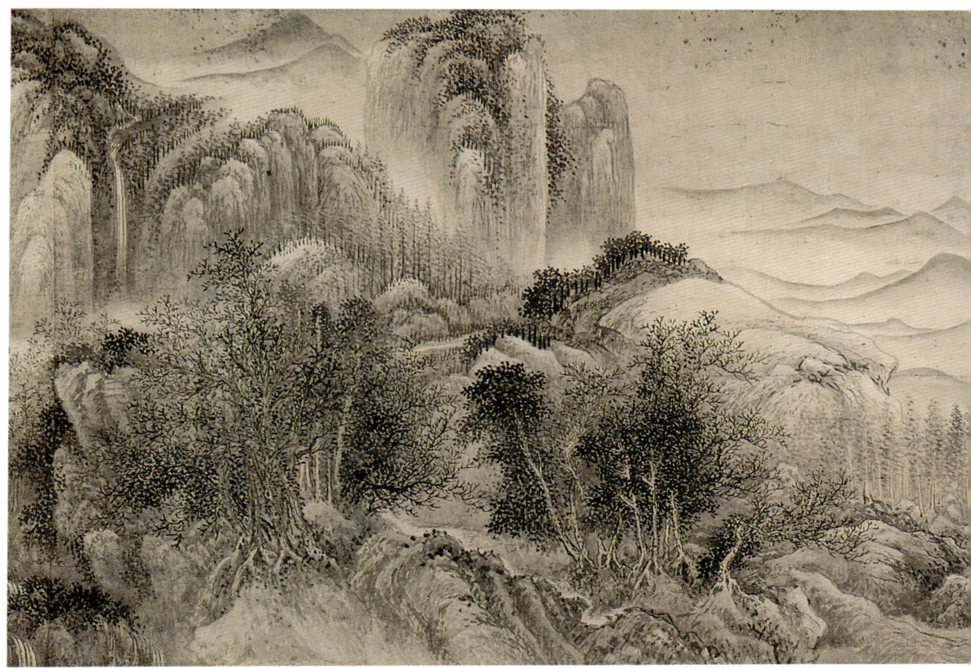

31. SUMMER MOUNTAINS, MISTY RAIN (DETAILS)

Wang Hui (1632–1717)
China; Qing dynasty, dated 1668
Handscroll, ink on paper
H: 43.8 cm (17¼ in.) W: 248.9 cm (98 in.)
87 D8
Gift of the Tang Foundation. Presented to the Asian Art Museum of San Francisco by Nadine Tang, Martin Tang, and Leslie Tang in honor of Jack C. C. Tang's sixtieth birthday.

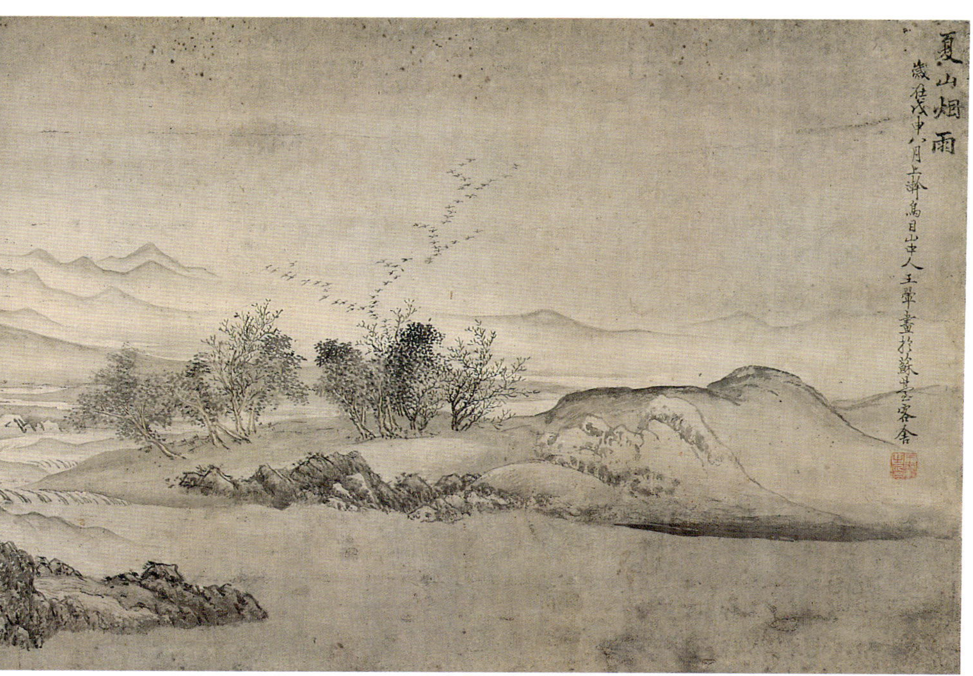

In 1668, Wang Hui changed the course of his career by painting the handscroll *Summer Mountains, Misty Rain.* The young artist had been working in Taichang under the patronage of Wang Shimin (1592–1677) and Wang Jian (1598–1677), the two eldest of the group of painters later called "the Four Wangs." But by the late 1660s, Wang Hui decided to broaden his horizons and seek the favor of Zhou Lianggong (1612–1672), the premier connoisseur of seventeenth-century China.[1] He painted *Summer Mountains, Misty Rain* as a presentation gift to Zhou, whom he had met several years earlier. It is his masterpiece to that date and evidence of his sense that Zhou Lianggong's patronage would alter his life. Zhou was engaged in his own life's work, a massive compendium of artists' biographies and highly personal criticism, the *Tuhualu* (Record of Paintings). Wang Hui must have known the value of a favorable mention in such a potentially influential work. As in many other instances in his life, he sealed the outcome with an adulatory colophon he solicited in 1669 from Wang Shimin, which recalls an earlier meeting between Wang Hui and Zhou Lianggong and the good feeling it generated.

Zhou Lianggong apparently greatly admired *Summer Mountains, Misty Rain*, for it bears several of his seals, showing he kept it in his collection. From 1669 until his death in 1672, he was Wang Hui's chief patron; his biography of Wang Hui in *Tuhualu* calls him "the greatest artist of the century." He introduced Wang Hui to his own wide circle of friends, sought his paintings avidly, and showed them to connoisseurs on his many travels. Zhou's

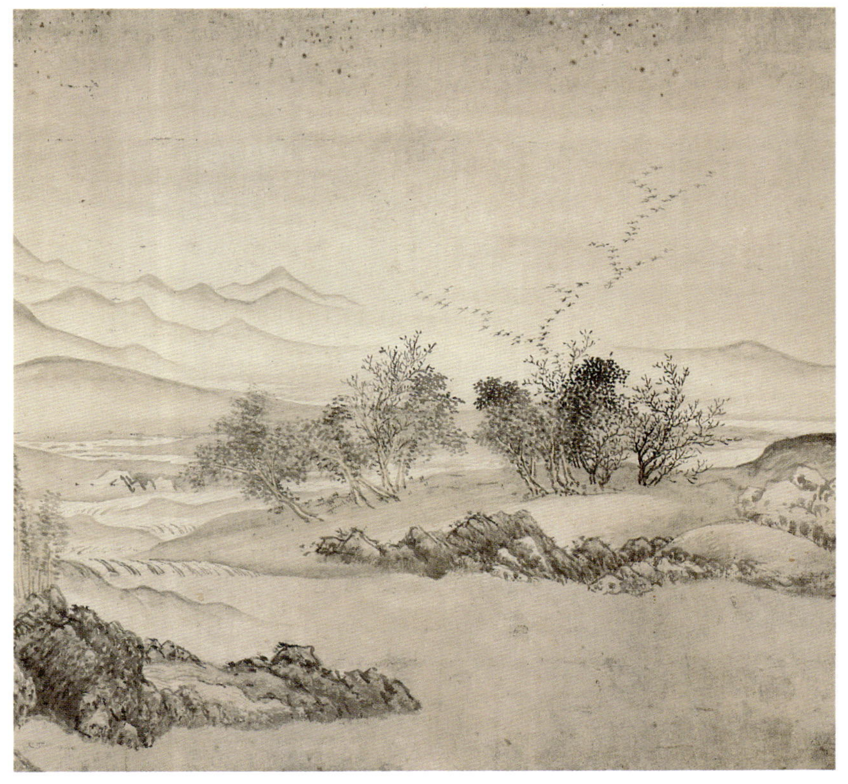

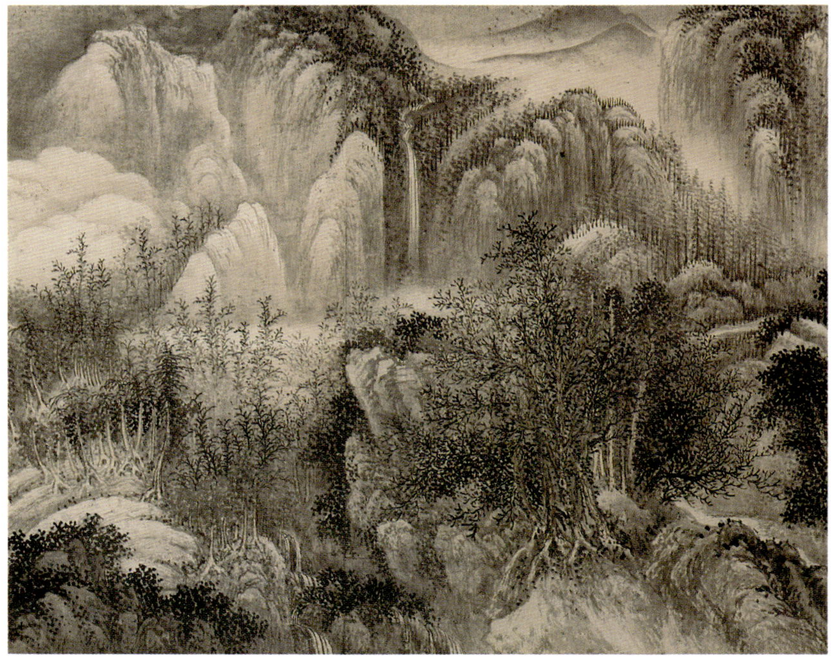

patronage eventually catapulted his protégé into a position of national prominence, so that in his old age Wang Hui was called to serve the Kangxi emperor (r. 1662–1722). He ended his career on a note of highly publicized virtuosity.

Summer Mountains, Misty Rain anticipates the more liberal artistic circles of Nanjing, and despite Wang Shimin's well-intentioned but inaccurate attempts in his colophon to fit it into the orthodox tenth-century tradition of Dong Yuan and Juran, it really owes more to the experimental landscape styles of the late Ming, especially the work of such masters of mood as Zhang Hong (1580–ca. 1660). Though the scroll still depends on the tradition of Song landscape painting, in its monumentally conceived composition, masterful draftsmanship, and engrossing detail, it also introduces much that is new. The fresh interest Wang Hui shows in the effects of light on form and its ability to clarify or veil detail is one he shared with other early Qing painters, including the individualist Gong Xian (active 1656–1682), a man who later became his friend. Wang Hui also demonstrates a virtuoso's talent for pictorial rhythms. He opens his handscroll with disarming simplicity—a flight of birds over an expanse of open water and rocks sketched in casually. He rapidly pulls his focus forward and mounts the composition to moody peaks, then diminishes, with cleverly disguised fluctuations of the horizon, to a gentle, moist scene of fishermen returning home along a marshy stream. His own inscription, at the beginning of the handscroll, is written in a style that evokes the imperial and scholarly calligraphers of the Song dynasty. It reads: "Summer Mountains, Misty Rain. Autumn of 1668, the eighth month, Wumu Shanzhongren [Crow's Eye Mountain Man, his nickname] Wang Hui of Shanghuan painted this in a Suzhou inn."

Wang Hui's personal seal follows his inscription. More seals of connoisseurs and collectors, including two belonging to Zhou Lianggong, appear at the end of the scroll. The long single colophon attached to the painting is Wang Shimin's famous notice of Wang Hui, published in his collected writings.[2] — P. B.

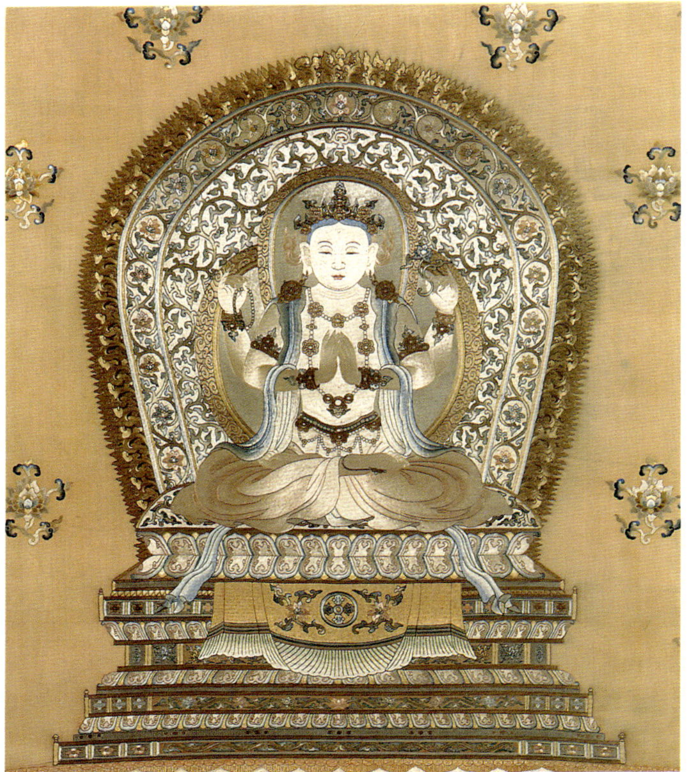

32. BODHISATTVA AVALOKITESHVARA (SHADAKSHARI-LOKESHVARA OR SIPI GUANYIN) (DETAIL)

China; Qing dynasty, Qianlong mark and period, 1736–1795
Hanging scroll, silk embroidery on silk ground
H: 209.5 cm (82 1/2 in.) W: 86.0 cm (33 7/8 in.)
1989.4
Gift of Walter and Phyllis Shorenstein

In an inscription written in 1744, when the Yonghe Palace was rededicated as a lamaist temple, the Qianlong emperor referred to his own father Yongzheng as King Shakyamuni, saying he had attained nirvana upon his death. The Yongzheng emperor had lived in the Yonghe Palace as heir-apparent; in its rededication, the princely hall where Qianlong himself was born became the center of lamaism in Manchu China. But by the end of his life, Qianlong was completely disillusioned with lamaism, especially with the Yellow Hat sect he had ensconced in the palace. He wrote in his eightieth year that his only reason for supporting the faith was to placate the devout Buddhists of Mongolia.[1]

Much too involved in his role as temporal ruler of China to favor one faith over another, Qianlong saw himself as an ecumenical patron who embodied the ideals of all religions. His support of different faiths was thus justified by political rather than spiritual needs. To demonstrate this concept, he enjoyed having his portrait painted in different roles—in Taoist robes, inserted into historical Buddhist scenes, and even transformed into a high lama, wearing a monk's patched robe and pointed cap and surrounded by a field of blossoms.[2]

Qianlong's own beloved mother, the Empress-Dowager Chongqing, was less cynical in her support of Buddhism. Her attentive son often gave her Buddhist icons as birthday presents, including a bronze lamaist pantheon consisting of 766 pieces.[3] Qianlong used luxurious devotional images, rendered in a polished Sino-Tibetan style and an incomparable courtly technique, as gifts that would inspire awe and compliance in potential allies as well. This image, which bears several of the emperor's own seals, was probably such a gift, intended for a high lama of the Yellow Hat sect. Its composition is identical to at least two other pieces, one in the Potala Palace in Lhasa, a gift to the Dalai Lama,[4] and the other in the National Palace Museum, Taipei.[5] All three are stamped with an assortment of the emperor's seals. The Potala scroll is rendered in the *kesi* slit tapestry technique with a heightened color scheme, but the Palace Museum scroll is nearly identical to the present piece, embroidered in a finely wrought satin stitch and couched silk thread in a palette confined to the palest pink, blue, and gold. There are only slight differences in color choice in some details.

The image represents the bodhisattva Avalokiteshvara, in his four-armed form as Shadakshari-Lokeshvara, or Lokeshvara of the Six Syllables, a reference to the prayer most closely identified with him, *Om Mani Padme Hum* (All Hail the Jewel in the Lotus). He is white, jeweled, and serenely seated in the lotus position on a sumptuously budding lotus throne, with two of his four hands in a gesture of offering at his heart. The right hand of the other pair holds a rosary, the left a lotus. The bodhisattva is shown against a field of lotuses, with the prayer *Om Mani Padme Hum* inscribed in bold cobalt blue Sanskrit above. Below, another prayer in Tibetan reads: "Fortunate days, fortunate nights, days and nights forever fortunate. Rely on the Three Jewels for good fortune."[6]

This Lokeshvara, like its mates in Lhasa and Taipei, was probably made before Qianlong's final disillusionment with the lamas of the Yellow Hat sect. An embroidered scroll described as Sipi Guanyin (Four-armed Guanyin) appears in the supplement to the catalogue of his collection, *Bidian Zhulin*; this is the scroll now in the National Palace Museum, Taipei. Next to it, another version in *kesi* tapestry is listed, perhaps the version now in the Potala. These two scrolls and the embroidered scroll in the Asian Art Museum all bear the *Bidian Zhulin* seal, meaning they at least passed through the imperial collection. The *Bidian Zhulin* supplement was published with an imperial preface dated 1793, near the end of the Qianlong reign, but its basic volumes first appeared in 1743.[7]—P. B.

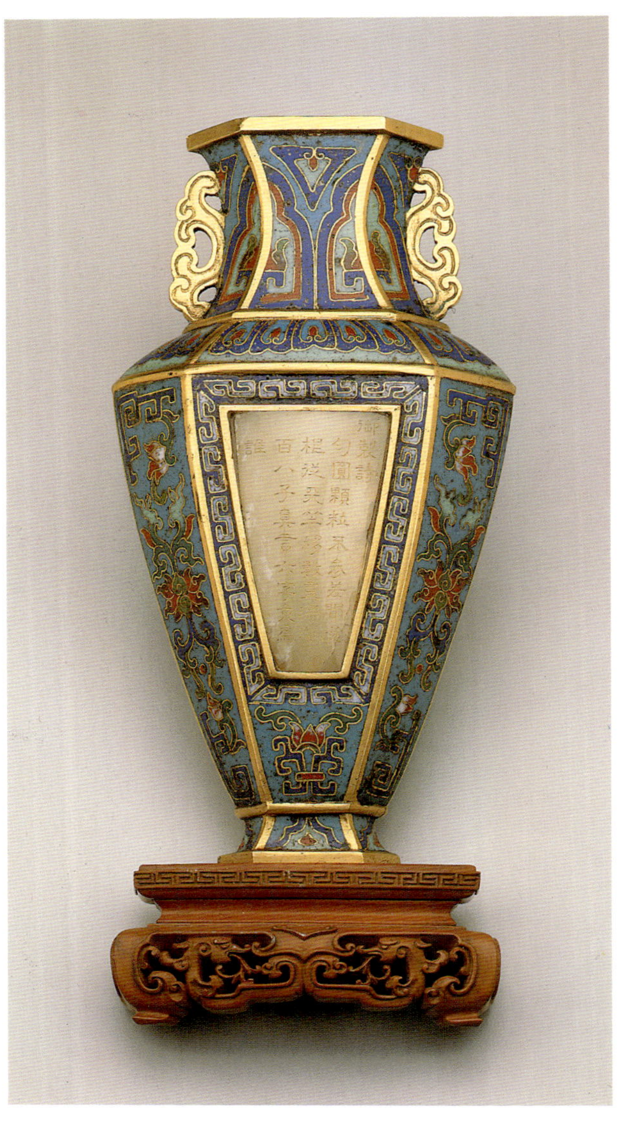

33. HALF-VASE

China; Qing dynasty, Qianlong period, 1736–1795
Cloisonné enamels on gilt bronze with jade inlay
H: 21.6 cm (8½ in.) W: 8.9 cm (3½ in.)
86 M8
Gift of Alexis Pencovic

The Qing emperors from Kangxi to Qianlong (1666–1795) were fascinated with science and avidly supported experimentation in the technical arts of enameling and glassmaking. European Jesuit enamelers were welcomed at court and encouraged to perfect opaque enamels, eventually achieving the *famille rose* palette, first developed by the Leiden physician Cassius.[1] Unlike the traditional cloisonné enamels of Ming China, these colors could be mixed with white to produce a wide palette of colors that emulated the shades of the painter in oils.

Under the patronage of the Qianlong emperor, however, traditional cloisonné enamels also underwent a revival. The style was strongly associated with the great reigns of the early Ming dynasty, and Qianlong's interest in it reflected his own view of himself as the rightful successor to those lines. Court-sponsored experiments with enamels had led to an improvement in cloisonné colors as well; the typical rose of the *famille rose* palette appears alongside more traditional colors, and the pitting that plagued Ming enamels is largely eliminated. Despite these technical improvements, the mood of Qing cloisonné enamels is archaizing; the motifs and their arrangement intentionally hark back to the early cloisonnés of the Ming.

This half-vase may have been one of a pair designed for use in a palanquin, an indication of the high level of decoration sustained during the Qianlong reign. It is inset with a jade plaque—a favorite combination of the Qianlong period—and inscribed with one of the thousands of lamentable poems composed by the emperor himself. Referring to the prayer *Om Mane Padme Hum* and to the devotional function of most early cloisonné enamels, which were designed for use in Buddhist and Taoist temples, he writes:

> Even and round, these prayer beads are unflawed.
> I have heard they come from India.
> When counted they number 108.
> For whom does one say the six true syllables?

—P. B.

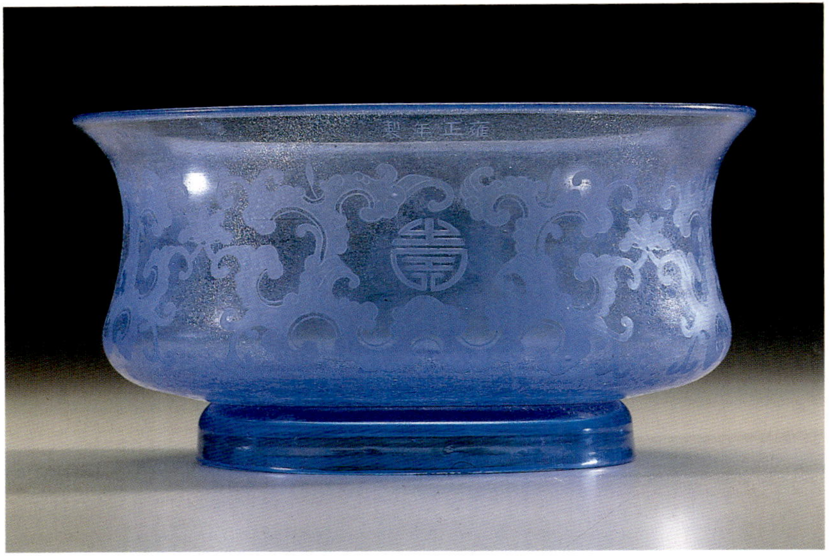

34. BOWL WITH CLOUDS, LOTUSES, AND "LONG LIFE" CHARACTERS

China; Qing dynasty, Yongzheng mark and reign, 1723–1735,
made at the Imperial Glass Studios, Beijing
Pale blue, clear glass with wheel-engraved designs
H: 9.0 cm (3⅝ in.) Diam: 17.3 cm (6⅞ in.)
87 M7
Gift of Dr. Jules and Hilda Koch

The Manchu rulers were exceptional patrons of the arts during their long reign (1644–1912). The Kangxi emperor in particular initiated an enduring program of art patronage, founding the Department of Public Artworks (Zaobanchu) in 1683. Located within the precincts of the Forbidden City, this department consisted of a series of specialized ateliers for the best craftsmen, painters, sculptors, carvers, and calligraphers throughout China. It promoted regional crafts and industrial and fine arts while encouraging assimilation of the latest inventions of the Western world.

In 1696 an imperial glass workshop was established in Yangxin Hall in the Forbidden City. Glassmaking in China came to prosper and flourish in a kind of golden age during the eighteenth century, as a result of the Manchu rulers' profound interest in it, which consequently influenced its local production for the court.[1]

The distinctive form of this bowl originates in early fifteenth-century Ming porcelain traditions; the type was revived in the eighteenth century. It has a flaring mouth, a rounded bottom, a pronounced foot ring, and a pinched waist to facilitate grasping. Known as *qingshuiwan* (pure water bowl), the shape is specifically that of an offering bowl in Buddhist ritual. Its decorative motifs, the lotus—symbolic of the essence of Buddha—and the Chinese character for long life (*shou*), carry the message of the endurance of the Buddhist faith.

This bowl was mold-blown; its rough pontil mark is still apparent. The foot ring was blown separately and heat-fused in a form and technique used in contemporary Venetian and North European lowland glass. It resembles an inverted shallow dish and displays a distinct curved contraction at the edge where the foot joins the bowl. While no precedent occurs in China's glass history for this peculiar convention, the technical antecedent is obviously Venetian-style European glass, documented to have entered China through the trade port of Guangzhou (Canton).[2]

This rare imperial-commissioned bowl is one of six known Yongzheng-marked glass vessels in American collections, and the only one having engraved decoration applied in a technique approximating Venetian diamond-tip etching.[3] Emulating the highly esteemed Venetian technique, the Chinese glassmaker decorated this bowl with the wheel-engraving discs used in jade-working studios; lateral traces of grinding are readily visible in the decorative band girdling the bowl.

The surface of this bowl has been affected by "crizzling," a technical term describing its silvery, powdery surface decomposition.[4] The cause lies in an unbalanced alkaline glass mix, a chemically unstable state reactive to relative humidity. Crizzling can indicate both authenticity and dating of early Qing Chinese glass, as it does not occur on Ming or Qing glass made after 1740.[5] The time span between the creation of the imperial glass house and 1740 parallels the time when European glassmakers were also working with chemically unstable glass formulas. It is believed that the "disease" was introduced to China from Europe, based on the records of George Stanton, eighteenth-century British ambassador to Beijing, who wrote of the Chinese glassmakers' practice of remelting broken European glass, thus contaminating the new batch. —C.F.S.

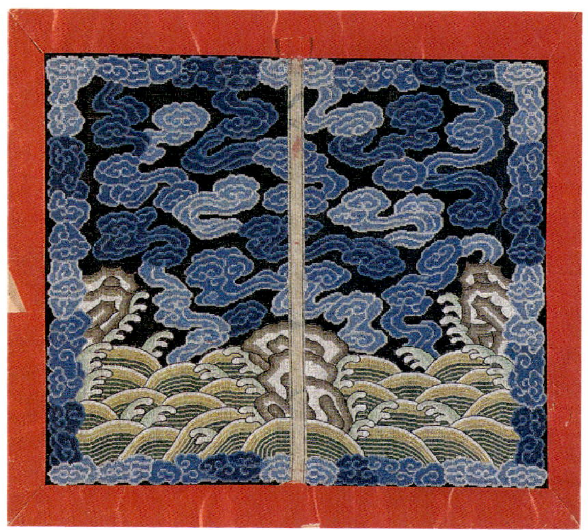

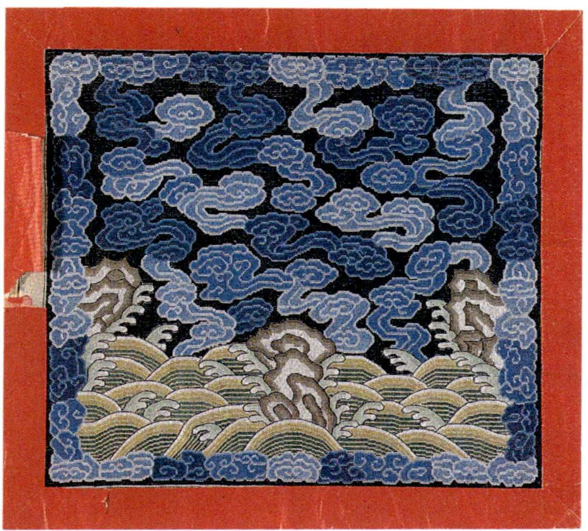

35. SET OF RANK BADGE BLANKS

China; Qing dynasty, late 19th century
Kesi (slit silk) tapestry in original red paper packaging
H: 26.6 cm (10½ in.) W: 28.2 cm (11⅛ in.)
1988.32.9a–b
Gift of Mrs. Ursula Bingham

No art form brings the viewer closer to its original patron than clothing. In Qing dynasty China, there were at least two kinds of costume: informal attire, which could effectively project individual taste, and formal wear, which was strictly regulated.[1] At the height of the Qing dynasty, in 1754, the Qianlong emperor instituted a rigorous dress code for the officials of his empire and for his imperial relatives. All attendants at court were robed in dark surcoats emblazoned front and back with rank badges that identified their position in the official hierarchy. There is every evidence that these badges were well earned and honestly worn through the end of the eighteenth century, but with the slow collapse of Manchu rule in the nineteenth century, the system of court patronage became eroded and corrupt. Ranks in both the military and civil services could be purchased, lists of their costs were broadcast by eunuchs of the imperial household, and specialists in rank-badge production proliferated, producing badges with fully worked backgrounds whose animal or bird symbols of military or civilian rank could be appliquéd in to speed the transition to higher office.[2]

This set of blanks is done in a *kesi* (slit tapestry) technique typical of the nineteenth century. The work is technically fine, but the smallest details have been added with brush and ink, an expedient often seen in later *kesi* tapestries. The front badge is slit to allow for the opening of the formal court surcoat, or *pufu*, and the central section of each badge has been left empty, allowing for the addition of the symbol of the wearer's civil or military rank. This commercialization of the original badges of rank continued until the end of the dynasty in 1912. By then, badges were often blindingly couched in threads of gold and silver, a manner court conservatives considered vulgar.

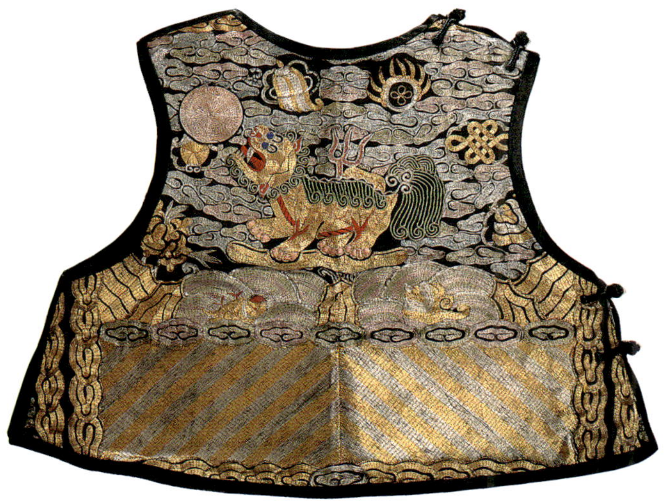

36. CHILD'S VEST

China, Qing dynasty, mid-19th century,
resewn early 20th century
Pair of rank badges couched in gold and silver
and lined in cotton
H: 28.0 cm (11 in.) W: 37.6 cm (14¾ in.)
86 M16
Gift of Dr. and Mrs. R. E. Sandlin

This mass of often-fine needlework was not discarded with the fall of the Qing dynasty. The badges were avidly collected and, as in this vest for a small child, reused in a way that suggests a lingering nostalgia for imperial times as well as extraordinary hopes for a young son. The vest is constructed of an original set of military badges of the first rank, identified by the lion, which has been appliquéd onto a set of all-purpose blanks embroidered with the eight Buddhist symbols (conch, fish, sun, wheel, lotus, knot, parasol, and canopy), useful for an official of any rank or category. The fine gold and silver couching, tacked down with threads of different colors to produce subtle changes of tone, is typical of the turn of the century. The split badge intended for the front of the court surcoat has been stitched together and used for the back. The new garment was then lined in simple blue cotton, suggesting that its proud wearer may have had an otherwise ordinary wardrobe.

The spring green "wedding" skirt, actually the ordinary informal skirt of a nineteenth-century gentlewoman, suggests much more about its wearer, since clothing worn in private was only subject to fashion, not code. The fabric is an exquisitely woven silk Han damask, whose warp-faced plain weave ground is decorated with warp floats that form a pattern of butterflies, decorated balls, and orchids.[3] But the sophistication of the weave is cleverly played off against a second pattern, done in wax resist, a technique with folkish associations, suggesting that its wearer was a young woman of unusual taste and interests. —P. B.

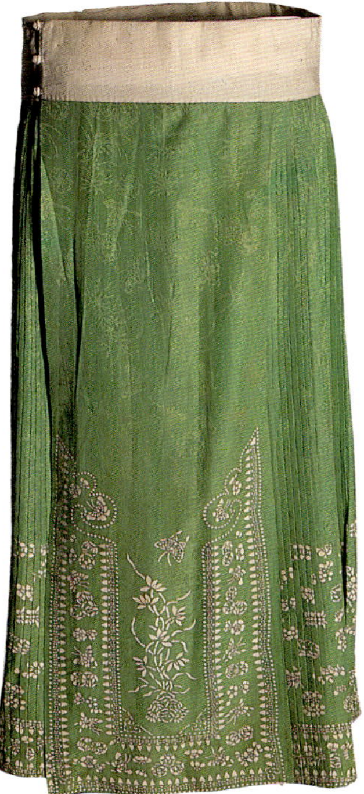

37. "WEDDING" SKIRT

China, Qing dynasty, late 19th century
Green silk damask with wax resist design
L: 92.7 cm (36½ in.)
W: (at hem) 299.7 cm (118 in.)
1988.32.26
Gift of Mrs. Ursula Bingham

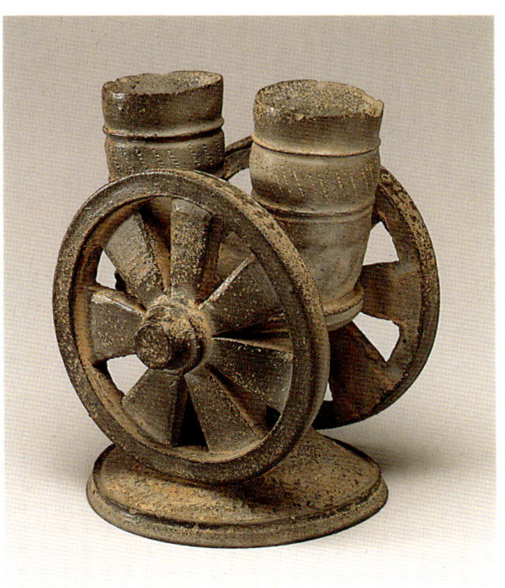

38. WHEELED CART WITH TWO JARS ON PERFORATED STAND

Korea; Three Kingdoms period, Kaya, 5th–6th century
Stoneware with traces of natural ash glaze
H: 10.4 cm (5½ in.)
1988.42
Gift of the Connoisseur's Council

This piece represents what may be a water cart with two wheels. On it are two tall jars connected at the base and bound together with a cordlike band on the outside. The cart is supported by a short, perforated pedestal. The pedestal and upright jars appear to have been made on a potter's wheel, while the wheels were cut from a slab of clay and attached to the sides of the cart.

Seven other Korean vessels of similar shape on wheeled carts have survived, and all are believed to have come from large tombs located near the lower reaches of the Naktong River in Kyŏngsang Province.[1] During the Three Kingdoms period (57 B.C.–A.D. 668) this area was under the control of a small confederation of tribes known collectively as the Kaya (42–562). It seems that they had direct sea trade with both Japan and China until they were annexed by the Old Silla Kingdom in 562.

Within Kaya territory it was common practice, as in the neighboring Old Silla Kingdom, to bury the leaders of their society in large tombs, usually semisubmerged rectangular pits, with stone-lined walls. After various items, such as food, jewelry, weapons, and pottery utensils, were placed in the tomb for use in the afterlife, the tomb was sealed under a large mound of earth that formed a tumulus. This piece was probably found among such grave goods. Although the exact function of these wheeled carts can never be proven, one Korean archaeologist suggests that they were intended as vehicles for the soul in the next world.[2] —R.M.

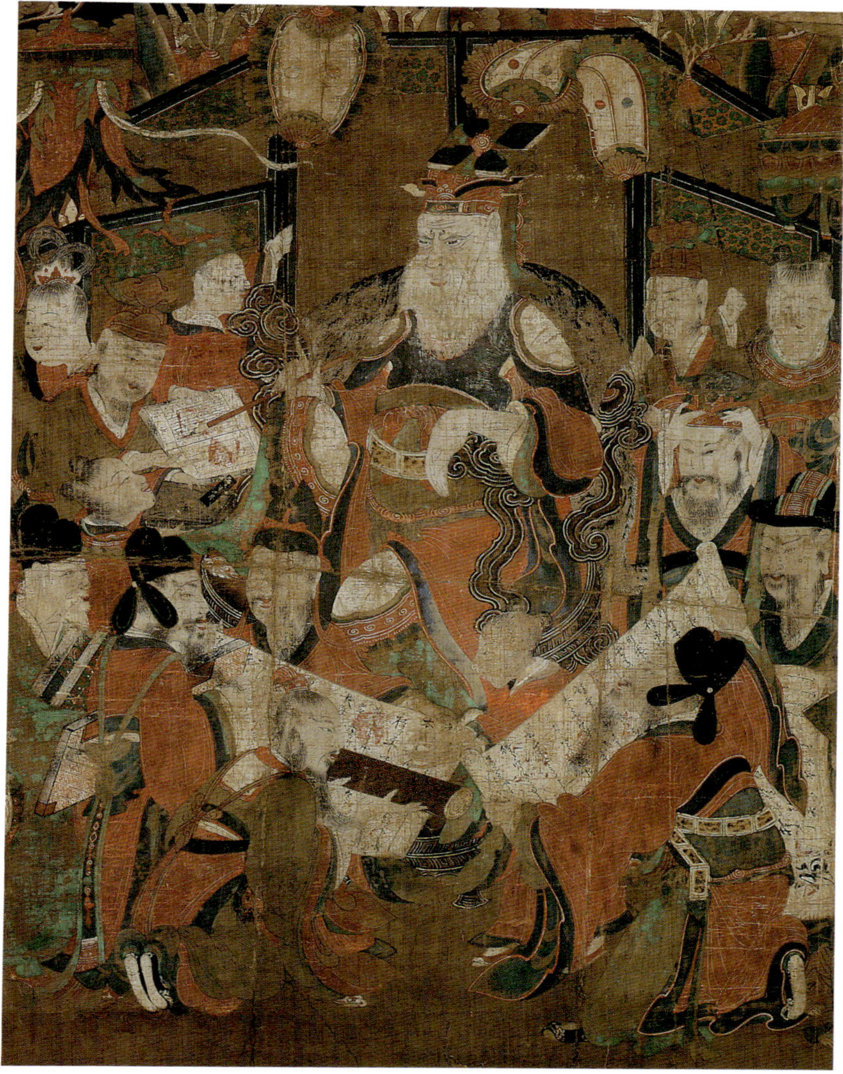

39. A KING OF HELL

Artist unknown
Korea; early Chosŏn period, 15th–16th century
Hanging scroll, ink and colors on silk
H: (painting only) 110.5 cm (45 1/4 in.)
W: 80.7 cm (34 1/4 in.)
86 D4
Gift of Dr. and Mrs. Sun-Hak Choy in honor of
Mr. James Dong-Wu Kim, Mrs. Choy's father

This painting depicts one of the Ten Kings of Hell seated on his throne and surrounded on three sides by servants, secretaries, and other officials. The cult of the Ten Kings of Hell probably entered Korea along with Buddhism during the late fourth century, and as in other countries of Asia, it underwent a process of cultural assimilation. Both Korean Buddhism and shamanism influenced the development of the Ten Kings. The cult has survived to the present: paintings of the kings of hell are usually enshrined in the Hall of the Deceased (Myŏngbu-chŏn) or in the King of Hell Hall (Yŏmna Taenang) at Buddhist monasteries. Shamans also sometimes own paintings depicting the same subject that they use in their rituals.

Korean Buddhist doctrine maintains that after death, the soul of a person rests in hell for forty-nine days. On the forty-ninth day the soul is brought before one of the kings of hell for judgment and sent either to everlasting paradise or to a place in hell. For this reason, on that final day most Korean families hold a memorial service in the Hall of the Deceased to attempt to influence the decision. Buddhist priests are hired to chant prayers, or sometimes a possessed shaman, or *mansin,* is asked to intercede on behalf of the deceased to ease the passage of the soul out of hell and into paradise.

Most king of hell paintings have a torture scene in the foreground which helps identify the king depicted. This painting lacks such a scene and therefore leaves his identity uncertain.

Korean Buddhist paintings often have a cartouche at the lower edge in which is written the date of the painting, the donors who commissioned and paid for it, the monks of the temple where it was installed, the temple for which it was painted, and sometimes even the artists who executed the work. Because this painting has been trimmed on all four sides, the cartouche has unfortunately been lost. We can therefore only theorize that, like most other Korean Buddhist paintings, this one was done at the request of a specific patron to help obtain salvation for a recently deceased loved one.

Painted with ink and colored mineral pigments on several vertical lengths of silk which have been sewn together, the composition is brilliantly conceived. Attention is cleverly focused on the king by the placement of the figures and the screen in the background. The king is larger in scale than any of the other figures; he sits on his throne isolated against a folding screen. The animated figures to either side, painted as distinct individuals, stand attentively ready to assist the king. The two officials in the foreground hold open handscrolls that create strong diagonals to help prevent the viewer's gaze from exiting the painting at the bottom.

Early in the Chosŏn period (1392–1910), belief in the Ten Kings was widespread. However, very few old paintings of the same subject have survived to the present, which makes accurate dating of this work extremely difficult. From stylistic features and the strength of the composition and draftsmanship, we can tentatively attribute it to the sixteenth century.
—R.M.

贈參判金公墓誌
金君美卿葬于牛耳里余嘗識其墓曰賢而
不得其年位理宜食報于其後書于石以俟
之以其子一聖集在耳越四年庚寅聖集又
夭繼葬于其左十步地嗚呼無可俟矣理其
可恃乎其母哭而謂余曰吾兒端詳孝謹簡
潔昭朗讀書能强記當事多精敏吾見人家
子雖不及吾兒亦多長成生育者獨使吾兒

40. EPITAPH TABLET (MYOJI)

Korea; Chosŏn period, 18th century
Porcelain with blue cobalt characters, glazed
H: 10.9 cm (7 1/2 in.) W: 10.4 cm (5 3/8 in.)
S1988.112
Gift of Mr. Arthur Leeper

The custom of writing an epitaph on stone or ceramic for placement in a tomb is an ancient one. In China, square stone plaques with incised inscriptions exist from as early as the Eastern Han period (23–220), while the earliest recorded epitaph in Korea is from the tomb of King Munyŏng (d. 523) of the Paekche dynasty (18 B.C.–A.D. 660). Tombs with epitaph tablets from the Three Kingdoms period (57 B.C.–A.D. 668), Unified Silla period (668–918), and Koryŏ period (918–1392) are for the most part those of royal family members, government officials, and other wealthy individuals. Beginning in the Chosŏn period (1392–1910), however, the custom of writing tablets about the dead was not only continued by government officials but was taken up by people of lesser rank.

The epitaph usually records the individual's name, official title or rank, birthplace, dates of birth and death, place of the family register, brief biography and eulogy, children, important relatives, and a dedicatory verse. Chosŏn-period epitaph tablets were made in several types of ceramic: a stoneware body with a celadon glaze and incised inscription, or a porcelain body with blue (cobalt) or brownish-black (iron oxide) writing covered with a translucent glaze. Typically there are four to six tablets in each set. Usually they are placed in a separate ceramic container and buried in the grave with the body.

This tablet has a notation on one edge that identifies it as the first of six tablets. The inscription reads:

> Presented in memory of Ch'amp'an Mr. Kim: Mr. Kim Migyŏng was buried at Wuyi-ri. I have something [to say about him] on the tomb. I say that he was wise and yet did not live long. It would be fitting that he be rewarded [through his children]. I wrote on this tomb [hoping to see this happen], because he had a son, Sŏngjip. Four years later Sŏngjip also died young in 1710 [or 1770] and was buried on the lot about ten steps [from his father's grave]. Alas, now there is nothing to wait for. It would have been good to have been able to wait [to see Mr. Kim rewarded]. [Sŏngjip's] mother wept and told me:
>
> "My son was upright, careful, filial, attentive, short and sweet [in his explanations], and bright and cheerful. He could remember clearly what he studied and undertook [other] matters carefully and sensitively. I saw sons of other families not as good as my son, and yet they all grow up and have children. Only my son used . . . ."[1]

—R.M. and K.K.

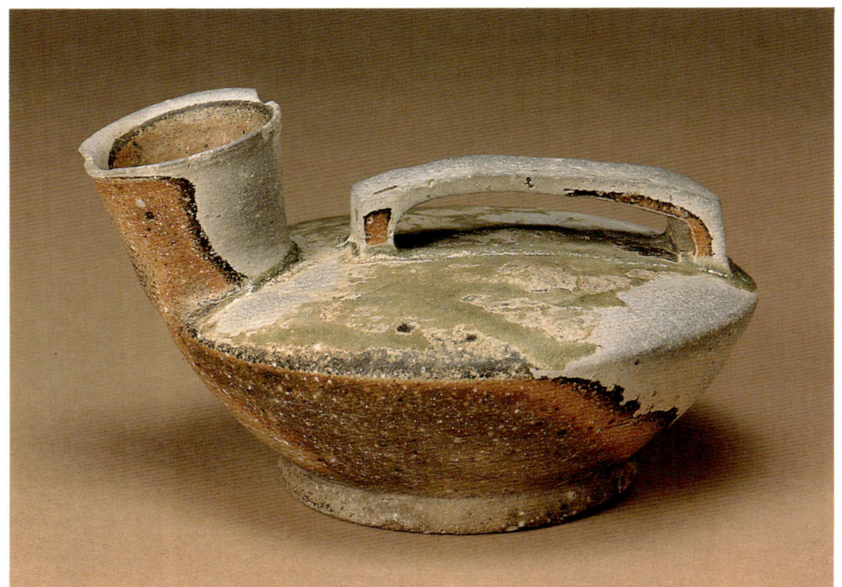

41. HEIHEI FLAT PITCHER WITH HANDLE

Japan; Heian period, from the Sanage kilns, ca. 800–850
Stoneware with ash glaze
H: 8.2 cm (3¼ in.) Diam: (of body) 13.3 cm (5¼ in.)
87 P2
Purchase: Asian Art Museum General Acquisitions Fund

This type of *heihei* (flat jar) evolved from flat-bottomed, spouted Sue ware jars of the Kofun and Nara periods (mid-third to late eighth centuries). This evolution of the form coincided with important technological advancements in the production of ceramics, which took place during the late Nara period. Up to this time, Sue ware was the only stoneware produced in Japan. It closely resembled Korean ceramics of the Three Kingdoms period (57 B.C.–A.D. 668), from which it derived. Typically Sue ware was unglazed and dark gray in color, but depending upon the clay composition and the method of firing, the color could range from almost black to reddish brown. Also, some pieces acquired areas of natural ash glaze on their surfaces, a glaze formed accidentally when wood ash fell on the vessels during firing. The differences between Sue ware and this deliberately ash-glazed *heihei* result from several technical features and the preferences of the clientele for whom they were made.

During the early decades of the eighth century, Sue potters working in Owari Province (present-day Aichi Prefecture) near Mount Sanage began experimenting with the purposeful application of ash glaze to the surface of pots. It is probable that requests from the central government, together with samples of Chinese ceramics with a light green glaze, prompted these experiments. By mid-century the potters had discovered a large deposit of superior clay near the base of Mount Sanage; this clay could withstand the temperature of 1240°C needed to mature an ash glaze. In order to further refine this clay, they began levigating it in shallow pools of water to reduce impurities in the body. This process not only made the resulting fired clay body lighter in color, but also increased the clay's plasticity. As a result of these and other developments, potters in this area began to produce the first high-fired ash-glazed ceramic ware in Japan.[1]

The new type of glazed ware was generally called *shiki* (glazed ware, a Chinese term). This term included another type of ceramic produced during this period, with a green glaze using copper for color and lead for a flux. Both these wares were copies of the much treasured and sought-after Chinese imports. One document from the late Heian period lists both these new types as highly desirable, calling them simply *ao-shi* (green ware) and *shira-shi* (white ware).

Construction techniques also changed, probably through the use of better potters' wheels. Separate parts were thrown and joined to make more complex forms. In fact, other forms of ash-glazed ware, such as water flasks, had been inspired by the crisp forms of bronze vessels. This *heihei* is made of at least three separate parts: body, neck, and handle, with a thrown-on foot.[2] An irregular green ash glaze covers the top, and a reddish brown glaze covers part of the spout and lower body. The piece is in a nearly perfect original state except for bare areas, which are likely the result of years of burial in the earth; the excavation site is unrecorded but was probably the user's residence.[3]

Pitchers of this type were used to serve beverages (smaller ones were used as water-droppers) in the palaces and homes of the wealthy, as well as in shrines and temples.[4]

Ware from the Sanage kilns was used for tribute payment to the palace and to the major temples. Later it was made specifically to fill orders placed by the government.[5] Thus Sanage's prosperity was partly a result of its proximity to good and abundant clay deposits, but owed more to the emergence of an affluent population that demanded and could afford such products. In a newly stabilized imperial court at the Heijō Palace, priests and government officials longed, in distant central Japan, for Chinese imports and ceramics in their style. All these factors contributed to the unparalleled success of the Sanage potters. — Y.K. and R.M.

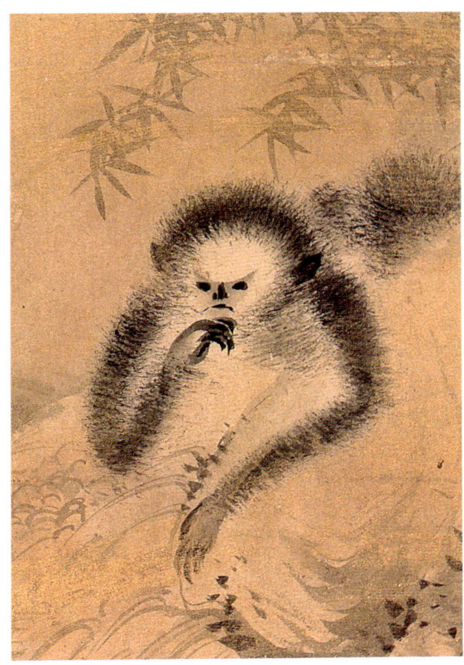

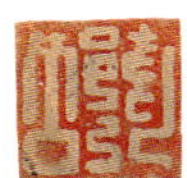

42. MONKEY (DETAILS)

Shikibu Terutada (fl. mid-16th century)
Japan; Muromachi period
Hanging scroll; ink and gold on paper
H: 19.3 cm (7 9/16 in.) W: 50.2 cm (19 3/4 in.)
1988.45
Gift of Mr. and Mrs. M. Glenn Vinson, Jr.

The monkey has long been popular in Chinese and Japanese painting; the most famous Chinese examples are those by Muqi, the Southern Song dynasty (1127–1279) painter. In Japan, Zen monk-painters of the Muromachi period (1392–1573) favored monkeys in Muqi's style, with round heads, long, thin limbs, and fur in repeated fine, dry brushstrokes.[1] This painting depicts a monkey thoughtfully peering over a cascading stream while lying on his stomach on a bluff. His pose derives from that of a monkey in a popular Buddhist painting, *Monkey Catching the Moon*, a parable about the discrepancy between truth and illusion. Bamboo leaves in varying ink tones subtly suggest space. At lower right is the artist's square intaglio seal, *Shikibu*.

Shikibu had fallen into obscurity by the seventeenth century, and errors subsequently plagued the attribution of his works. Only in recent years was he identified as a painter active in the mid-sixteenth century in the Kantō area, the eastern region around Kamakura. From stylistic evidence, it is thought that Shikibu belonged to the so-called Kamakura school.[2] A prolific painter, Shikibu excelled in works as large as screens and as small as fans, which he executed in a simple, abbreviated style. Although now composed as hanging scrolls, most of these fan paintings were originally mounted on folding screens.[3]

Fans have been popular in Japan for practical and ceremonial purposes since the Heian period (897–1185). Some Muromachi-period fans were produced as gift items appropriate for happy occasions. They were typically decorated by professional fan painters (*ōgiya*). As Chinese-style ink paintings became popular, fans were executed with monochrome ink paintings and were sometimes commissioned by feudal patrons.[4] Restrained and austere, they must have appealed to warrior-class taste and were much in demand; soon they became a profitable enterprise for ink painters.[5] Screens composed of mounted fans, with their varied subjects and the interesting effect of their shapes, were much appreciated for both ceremonies or interior decor.

Little is known of Shikibu's whereabouts or activities in the Kantō region. Circumstantial and stylistic evidence strongly suggests that he was at one time connected with the Kenchōji temple in Kamakura and most likely trained as a Zen monk and painter.[6] It is also thought that he learned his superior composition from Kanō Gyokuraku and Kōetsu, both painters of the Odawara Kanō school, who worked under the patronage of the powerful Hōjō family of Odawara.[7]

Hōjō So'un (1432–1519) founded the Hōjō family, and his descendants controlled the entire Kantō region including Kamakura until 1590. Shikibu's connection with Hōjō patronage is established by one of his paintings in the Sō'unji in Yumoto, a Zen temple erected by the Hōjō.[8] The family was known for its keen interest in art and literature, and they were patrons of the renowned *rengashi* Sōboku, of the Odawara Kanō school painters, and the great Zen monk-painter Sesson Shūkei (1504–1589). Shikibu's and Sesson's works for the Hōjō suggest the two artists were in Odawara about the same time.

While the specific patron for this monkey painting is not known, it exemplifies a kind of work done by Shikibu for warlord patrons, who were actively shaping their own art, which came to blossom a few decades later in the vigor and glory of the Momoyama period (1573–1615). —Y.W.

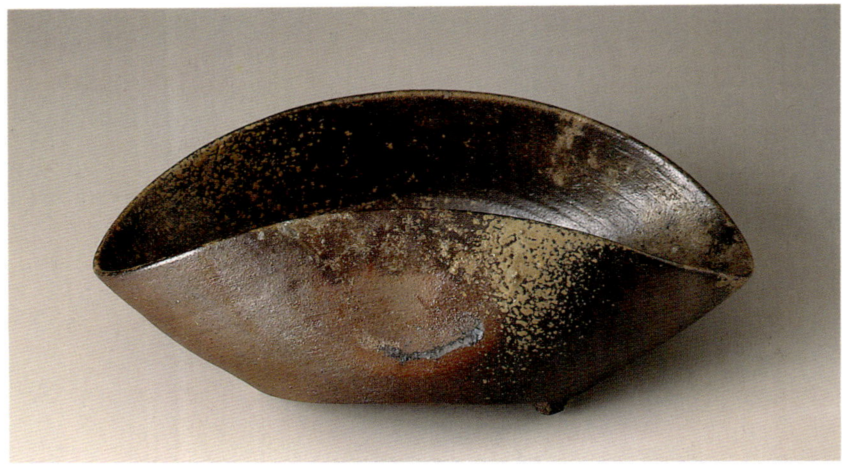

43. BIZEN BOWL

Japan; Momoyama period, late 16th century
Stoneware
H: 11.2 cm (4 3/8 in.) W: 15.9 cm (6 1/4 in.)
L: 28.9 cm (11 3/8 in.)
76 P4
Gift of William S. Picher

Chanoyu, ceremonial tea-drinking, is a Japanese cultural phenomenon so extraordinary it is without comparable observance in other cultures. Sen no Rikyū (1522–1591), probably the most famous of hundreds of distinguished practitioners of *chanoyu*, once described the essentials of the complex tea ceremony as "an act of boiling water and serving a bowl of tea." Why, then, did the simple act of making tea develop into such a complicated set of activities?

Volumes of written instructions, records,[1] and treatises exist as well as countless numbers of buildings called tea houses, all devoted to tea-drinking activities. These houses are usually equipped with a complex set of utensils for basic tea service as well as a reserve of other objects from which the host selects a combination appropriate for the specific surroundings and occasion.[2] This concept of regarding each occasion as singular (one and only, *ichigo ichie*), and necessitating a uniquely appropriate setting, appears to be among the key determinants of what *chanoyu* became. Today it is observed in the most recent stylistic form, which was established near the end of the sixteenth century.

When the custom of tea-drinking was first introduced from China during the Heian period (794–1185) and reintroduced during the Kamakura period (1185–1333), it involved consumption of a simple beverage sometimes regarded as having medicinal qualities. The practice was common in the court, and later among Zen priests. During the Muromachi period (1392–

1573), among the upper class, tea-drinking took the form of entertainment. Often gambling was the central theme of such parties, and bathing was a supplemental but important part of the enjoyment. The interior settings for these parties were mainly Chinese in taste, with many treasured imported utensils displayed, used, and given away as gambling prizes.

Around the end of the sixteenth century, Murata Jukō, his adopted son Sōju, and Take no Jōō, all from *machishū* (townspeople) families, changed *chanoyu* practice into something more spiritual. Before this time tea-drinking may have taken place in rooms ranging from the palatial to those of more modest size. Now, however, Jōō established the basic setting, the tea room, of four and one-half tatami mats (9 × 9 feet). It is said he wished to feel as if he were in a remote mountain forest while living in a crowded city, possibly a manifestation of his Zen meditative spirit. Jōō's student Rikyū, also a Zen practitioner and son of a Sakai merchant, is generally given credit for canonizing and popularizing Jōō's philosophy, now called *wabi no chanoyu* (tea of austere taste).

The tea house and utensils Rikyū used were tangible and visual manifestations of his tea aesthetics. He chose everyday Korean food bowls for tea bowls and treasured them for their most ordinary appearance in interiors that resembled humble farmhouses, some as small as two tatami (6 × 6 feet). He also used unglazed stoneware storage jars for water containers in the preparation room. They were usually strong and unadorned, with the kind of beauty described as *hieta* (cool).

In mid-career, Rikyū became concerned with the design of his tea bowls. In his quest for ideal utensils, he commissioned them from the potter Chōjirō, son of a Korean roof-tile maker, Ameya. His search produced a series of raku tea bowls handmade and fired one at a time, as if each were a piece of sculpture. These raku bowls were the essence of understatement. Rikyū, who also made his simple bamboo flower vases and tea scoops, was thus able to assemble a group of utensils to convey visually the aesthetics of his tea observance. His strong convictions inevitably caused conflict between him and his master, Toyotomi Hideyoshi (1536–1598). Hideyoshi, a self-made samurai general who became the political leader of Japan, was an individual of equally strong personality and a taste for ostentation. Rikyū, at the end, chose death when accused by Hideyoshi of disrespect, leaving the future of his teaching to his followers.

One of Rikyū's most devoted students, Furuta Oribe (1544–1615), a samurai by birth, introduced still different elements in his tea aesthetics. His name has been traditionally associated with the green glaze developed around 1600 in a fast-developing pottery center in Mino Province. Oribe chose colors brighter than the earthy range preferred by his master Rikyū; he used light colors, such as Shino and yellow Seto glazes, in his strong designs in which contrasting elements were often juxtaposed. Oribe combined black and green with a light, natural feldspar glaze, and decorated light areas with whimsical designs in iron-oxide slip to create striking design effects.

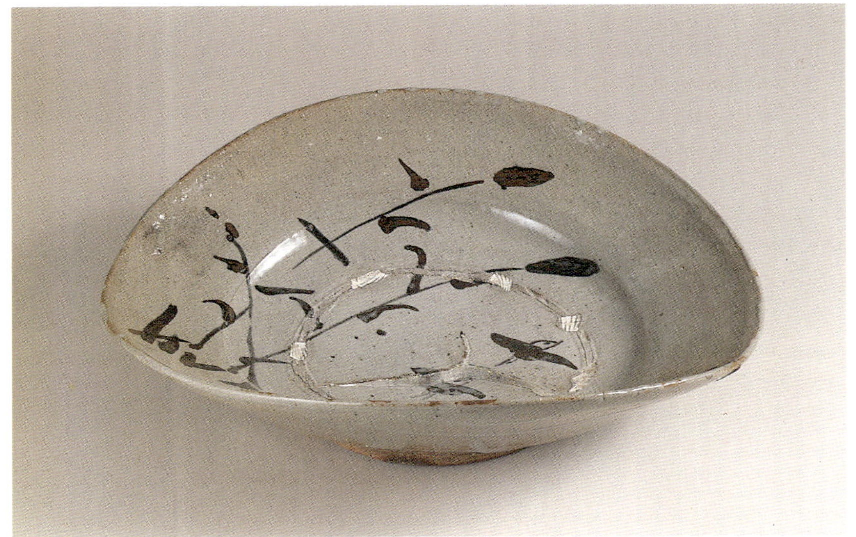

44. LARGE E-KARATSU BOWL

Japan; Momoyama period, late 16th century
Glazed stoneware with underglaze iron decoration
H: 12.4 cm ($4^{7}/_{8}$ in.) Diam: 41.9 cm ($16^{1}/_{2}$ in.
84 P1
Gift of Alice C. Kent

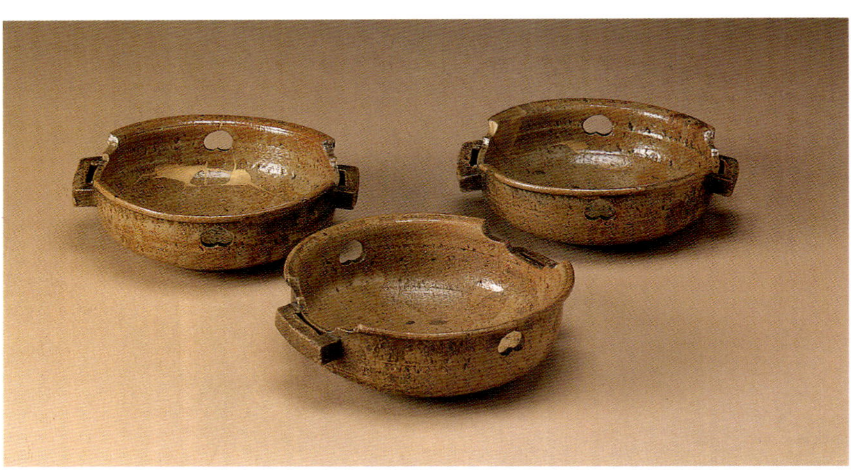

45. THREE KI-SETO MUKŌZUKE DISHES

Japan; Momoyama period, late 16th century
Glazed stoneware
H: 4.8 cm ($1^{5}/_{8}$ in.) W: (*1 & 2*) 13.0 cm ($5^{1}/_{8}$ in.),
(3) 12.7 cm (5 in.)
87 P11.1–3
Gift of James O'Brien

While his colors were strong, Oribe preferred irregular and sometimes nearly outrageous shapes. A typical example is a series of tea bowls called *kutsu-gata* (shoe-shaped); the wheel-thrown tea bowls, while still soft enough to be flexible, were pushed nearly oblong so as to resemble the wooden shoes (*bokuri*) worn with courtly garments. Records of tea ceremonies and diaries kept by Momoyama-period (1573–1615) tea practitioners list many such *hyōgemono* (misshapen ware) tea bowls.

This selection of stoneware vessels represents Oribe's taste for irregular shapes. The Bizen bowl was intended for the *kaiseki*, a meal served before tea at the tea-gathering. This one acquired its shape during firing when another piece in the kiln accidentally fell against it. The large E-Karatsu bowl cracked during firing. The piece was found interesting, saved and repaired, although crudely, by someone who shared Oribe's taste.[3]

Since Oribe was once stationed in Nagoya in northern Kyushu near Karatsu, during Hideyoshi's Korean peninsula campaign, it was quite probable that many tea practitioners who lived in the area as well as the Karatsu potters came into closer contact with Oribe's new tea aesthetic. The group of three yellow Seto (*ki-seto*) ware *mukōzuke* dishes (for *kaiseki*, serving marinated food) was once part of a set of five. These dishes have been repaired with gold lacquer. According to a perhaps exaggerated or embellished account, Oribe is said to have deliberately broken a rather ordinary bowl and had it mended in order to make it more interesting.[4] In any case, many individuals with strong preferences and convictions regarding the nature of the tea ceremony contributed to the unique complexities of its aesthetics. —Y.K.

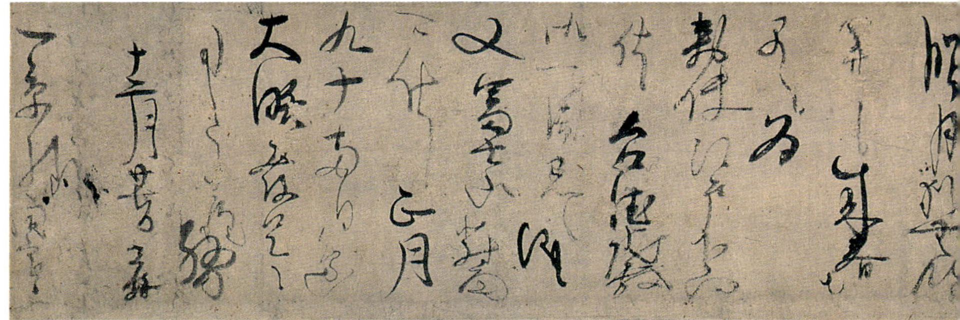

46. LETTER TO ISSHI MONJU

Karasumaru Mitsuhiro (1579–1638)
Japan; Edo period, datable to 1632
Hanging scroll, ink on paper
H: 15.9 cm (6¼ in.) W: 94.3 cm (37⅛ in.)
1988.28
Gift of Elizabeth and Allen Michels and an anonymous donor

This is a personal letter from a poet-calligrapher courtier, Karasumaru Mitsuhiro, to his young religious mentor Isshi Monju (1608–1646), a Rinzai sect Zen priest.[1] The Karasumaru family was a branch of the Fujiwara clan, the oldest and one of the most distinguished clans. Dating back to the seventh century, it had for generations served the imperial court as statesmen, poets, and calligraphers. Mitsuhiro, who was given a court rank at the early age of three, quickly ascended to high rank and served two emperors, Go-Yōzei (1571–1617), and Go-Mizunoo (1596–1680).

Mitsuhiro began training in calligraphy at eight years of age under his father, Karasumaru Mitsunobu, also a renowned calligrapher and poet. From his mid-twenties to mid-thirties, he studied calligraphy with Hon'ami Kōetsu (1558–1637), his contemporary and master of many artistic media. Mitsuhiro came to be called the Fourth Great Brush after the famous Three (Great) Brushes of the Kanei era, Kōetsu, Shōkadō, and Nobutada. By the last decade of his life, his personal style was recognized as Mitsuhiro *ryū*, or the Mitsuhiro style.

Mitsuhiro's letter shows a casual yet strong handwriting. He began the message in bold strokes on the right and progressed to the left, occasionally dipping his brush in ink, as indicated by running dark letters. Mitsuhiro expresses his anxiousness for Isshi's well-being and discusses his own pending trip to Edo as an envoy of Emperor Meishō to attend the first anniversary service of the late second shogun, Hidetada.[2] He looks forward to this trip and another chance to "face" or to "meet" Mount Fuji, favorite subject of many of his paintings and poems. After completing the message with the salutation and his signature, Mitsuhiro returned to the right margin to add

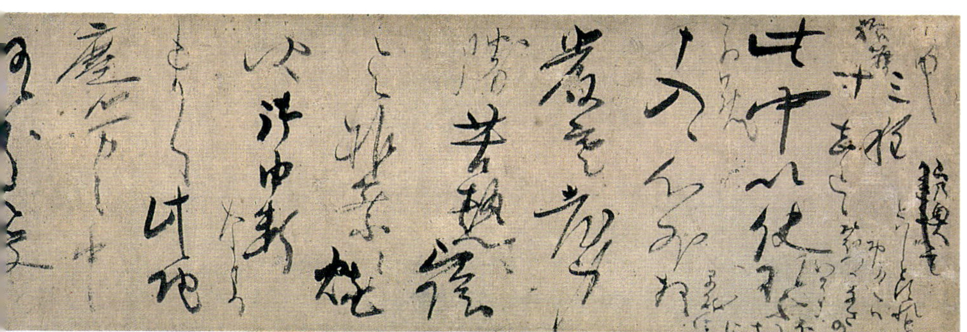

his *waka* poem. Full of concern for his young but frail mentor, who resided in a distant province known for its severe winters, it fills most of the right margin and spills into the space between lines of the letter.

In this brief letter Mitsuhiro captured the essence of courtly life in Kyoto during the reign of Emperor Go-Mizunoo, a ruler especially important in Japanese cultural history for having established the era now referred to as the Kanei culture, and for his lifelong artistic activities.[3]

Gradually stripped of political power by the expanding Tokugawa shogunate, Go-Mizunoo devoted himself to the study of traditional *waka* poems. He wrote many volumes on literature, poetry, and court ceremonies, and received a shogunal order to devote himself to the study of various arts as a guardian of court tradition.[4]

To the emperor Go-Mizunoo's courtiers and their religious leaders, such as Takuan (1573–1645) and Isshi, daily life was a subtle aesthetic and literary experience. Courtiers like Mitsuhiro not only studied with great artists but also patronized and sometimes collaborated with them.

Mitsuhiro collected earlier calligraphic works for study and enjoyment. His calligraphy, including his letters, has been treasured by later connoisseurs. This letter is mounted tastefully as a *chagake*, or scroll to accompany the tea ceremony, using a type of textile known as "water weave" to enhance the fluidity and delicacy of the calligraphy. — Y.K.

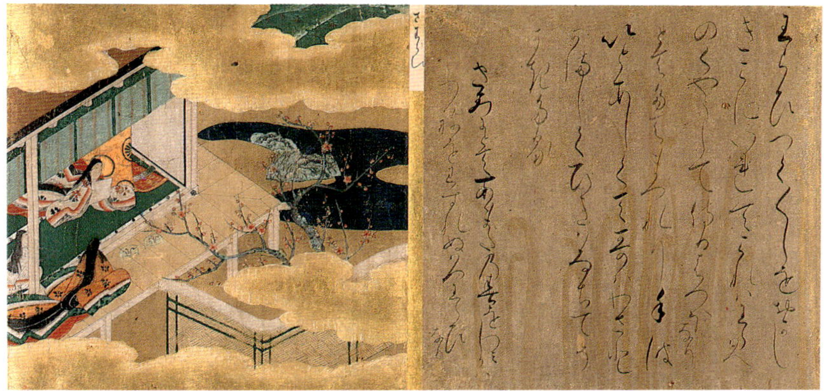

47. TALE OF GENJI (DETAIL)

Anonymous artists
Japan; Momoyama to Edo period, 17th century
Handscroll; ink colors, and gold on paper
H: 22.3 cm (8³/₄ in.) W: 22.3 cm (8³/₄ in.)
86 D2
Gift of the Walter and Phyllis Shorenstein Fund

This scroll contains twelve narrative sets, each consisting of a painting and a short accompanying text written on a decorated square paper called *shikishi*. Each set represents a scene from a chapter of the *Tale of Genji*, with the chapter title written in a small cartouche placed between the corresponding squares. Of the fifty-four chapters of the *Tale of Genji*, twelve are represented in this scroll.[1]

The *Tale of Genji*, written during the first decade of the eleventh century and later appearing in the form of an illustrated handscroll, is one of the world's most distinguished literary and artistic achievements. The author, Lady Murasaki, grew up in intellectual surroundings and received an education unusual for a woman—she learned the Chinese classics while her brother was being taught by their father.

Widowed while still young, Murasaki entered service at the imperial court, where she became a tutor to the powerful consort Shoshi, mother of the young Emperor Go-Ichijō. Both Murasaki and her literary work enjoyed the patronage of the entire court, including Shōshi's father, the powerful Fujiwara no Michinaga (966–1027).

From the time the chapters appeared, issued most probably in Murasaki's handwriting in the graceful *kana* script,[2] the *Tale of Genji* captured the imagination of the Heian court, whose members eagerly waited to learn the fate of the young princes and princesses, in whom they saw themselves reflected. The richness of Murasaki's narrative style (such tales were customarily read aloud) and the story's literary depth, with its underlying Buddhist philosophy, filled many a lonely heart among the less-privileged readers of subsequent eras.

Romances of the Heian period were usually illustrated by skilled artists, and the texts were often executed by famous calligraphers of high rank. The earliest and most celebrated examples of the *Genji* narrative now in Japanese collections are from the mid-twelfth century.[3] They are executed in the *onna-e* style (women's painting) with thick opaque pigment. The illustrations' richness is surpassed only by the elegance of the decorated paper on which the texts are written in *kana* script by five different calligraphers.

Many painters of later periods illustrated the *Tale of Genji* and found artistic inspiration in it. Later examples of the tale tend to have simplified texts, unlike the older versions. No doubt such simplification was required to meet the demand for versions of *Genji*, which soon became part of the basic literary library for the dowries of daughters of the wealthy. (By this period, patrons of such works had also become more numerous, but were of less elevated social rank.)

Among numerous books written about the *Tale of Genji* was the *Genji Monogatari Ekotoba*, a model book for painters and the calligraphers who worked with them. One version of this book, dating from the late sixteenth century, contains selected passages from a few scenes of each chapter. For each scene it provides information about such details as the season, costume colors, and especially the interior settings, as well as basic compositional arrangements of the main characters.[4]

Among the texts included in the Asian Art Museum scroll, those from Chapters 26, 29, 30, 31, and 48 closely parallel the *Ekotoba* scripts. In this painting, from Chapter 48, "Sawarabi" (Young Fern), the lady Nakano-kimi sits facing the garden, where a pink plum tree is in full blossom. On the *en* (the narrow covered deck next to the room) are two baskets of young fern shoots, a present from the priest who lives in the hills. A lady-in-waiting on the *en* and another just inside the room sit facing their mistress. The diagonal lines of the roofless building and the partial cloud-covers are typical devices of a *Genji* painting.

In composition, paintings of several chapters of this group closely resemble those of other famous published examples from the Momoyama period. However, the style of the paper decorations on their text squares seems to indicate a difference, perhaps in the date of execution or the purely individual taste of this particular artist and even possibly of the patron. Unlike the bold and strong Momoyama style with its familiar diagonal lines and gold flakes, these text decorations are soft and graceful, with occasional images pointing to themes from the story. One of the most beautiful appears on the text sheet of Chapter 48. The simple forms of the young fern shoots are painted with unpretentious brushstrokes. The relaxed depiction of the figures in some scenes also suggests a similar personal aesthetic. —Y.K.

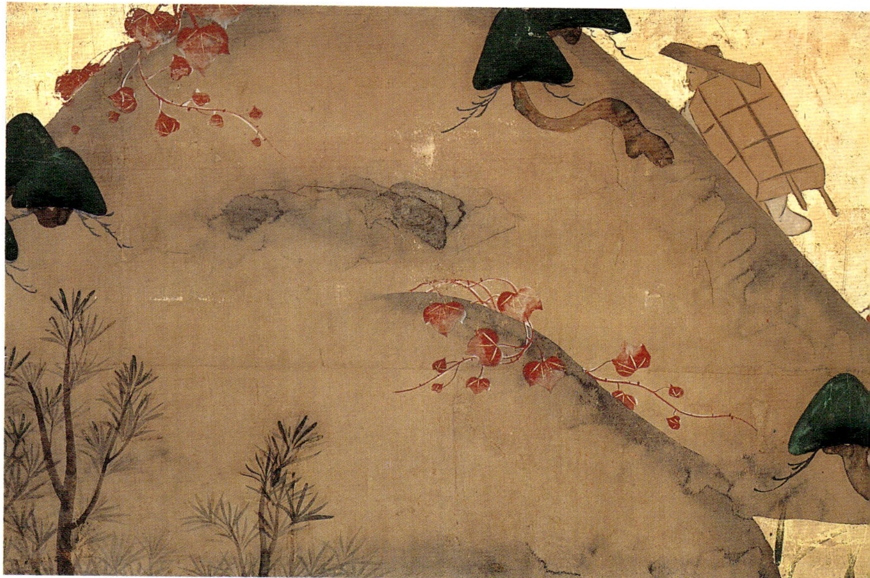

48. THE PATH THROUGH MOUNT UTSU (SCENE FROM THE TALES OF ISE)

Fukae Roshū (1699–1757)
Japan; Edo period, 18th century
Two-fold screen; ink, colors, and gold on paper
H: 61.6 cm (24¼ in.) W: 182.6 cm (71⅞ in.)
86 D3
Purchased through the Connoisseur's Council, the Asian Art Museum General Acquisitions Fund, and a gift of Elizabeth and Allen Michels

The *Tales of Ise*, the mid-tenth-century story of a courtier and his romantic pursuits, has provided themes of a literary nature to many Japanese painters. In their early development, scenes from the tales were depicted in a continuous narrative form in handscrolls. Later, single scenes were represented in screens and hanging scrolls. This screen depicts the famous ninth story, "The Path through Mount Utsu," or simply "Ivy Lane," where the hero in exile, Arihara no Narihira, appears in a blue garment against a landscape in which mountains close in on either side. He meets a traveling priest, whom he asks to deliver a letter to a woman he left in Kyoto. The ivy vine turning color indicates the season is autumn. The screen is signed *Fukae Roshū* and has a seal, *Roshū*.

Roshū is a painter of the Rimpa school, whose colorful decorative style derived from the painting tradition established in Kyoto by Tawaraya Sōtatsu (?–1643) and Ogata Kōrin (1658–1716). The scanty facts of Roshū's biography indicate that he was the first son of Fukae Shōzaemon, one of the four powerful officers in the mint of the Tokugawa shogunate in Kyoto.[1] Among Shōzaemon's colleagues was Nakamura Kuranosuke, Kōrin's patron, who was

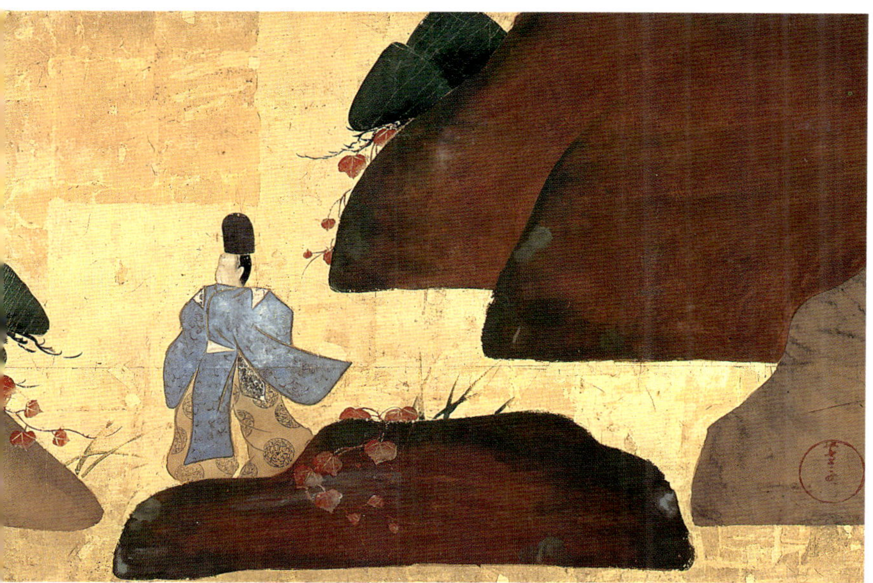

notorious for his extravagant life. Like other mint officers, Shōzaemon amassed a fortune through his work and carefully built up his properties. In private life he was a scholarly man, an ardent believer of Ōbaku Zen, and was the author of *Tsūkan Kōmoku.* The young Roshū must have known luxury and culture, but in 1714, he lost practically everything; his father was implicated in mismanagement of the mint, and with Nakamura Kuranosuke was exiled to the island of Miyakejima, where he died in 1718. Roshū's mother committed suicide, and Roshū was expelled from Kyoto. His life thereafter is obscure, probably due to his father's disgrace.

Roshū's twenty to thirty extant works reveal that he worked closely in the style and themes of the Rimpa school.[2] It is conjectured that the young Roshū studied painting under Kōrin, who was patronized by his father and Nakamura Kuranosuke, and that after Shōzaemon's fall from favor Roshū earned a living by selling paintings to affluent merchants in Kyoto.[3]

In the Edo period (1615–1867), the Japanese were categorized in a four-part class system—samurai, farmers, artisans, and merchants, in descending order of status. The demarcation between artisans and merchants was not clear; as city dwellers they were all called townsmen (*machishū* or *chōnin*). While lacking political power, *machishū* steadily accumulated great economic power. Their wealth gave them leisure to acquire learning, enjoy literary pursuits, and patronize arts; the more affluent had contacts with nobles of the court. Tawaraya Sōtatsu and Ogata Kōrin, both natives of Kyoto with merchant backgrounds, were patronized by court nobles and upper-class townsmen. Roshū's brilliantly designed flower and plant paintings and depictions from such classics as the *Tales of Ise* and the *Tale of Genji* indicate that his clients were basically the same as those of Sōtatsu and Kōrin. —Y. W.

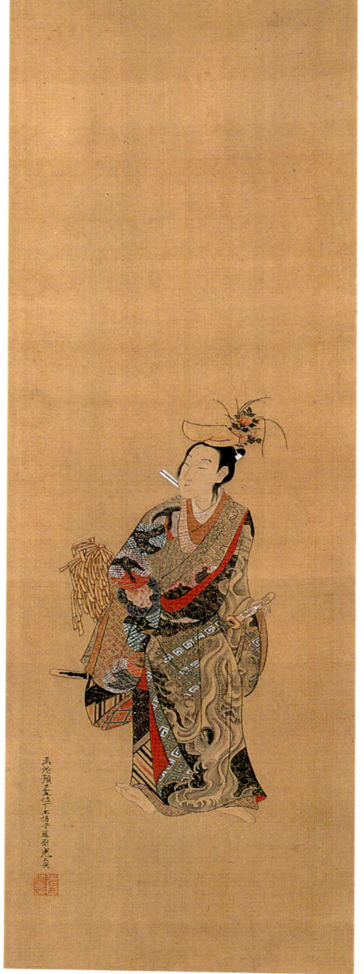

49. WAKASHŪ (YOUNG KABUKI DANCER)

Tosa Mitsusada (1738–1806)
Japan; Edo period
Hanging scroll; ink, color, and gold on silk
H: 91.0 cm (35⁷/₈ in.) W: 29.8 cm (11³/₄ in.)
1988.48
Purchased through a gift of Jane R. Lurie and the Asian Art Museum General Acquisitions Fund

This painting depicts a handsome young male dancer dressed in the elaborately decorated costume for *Daishō no mai* (Dance of Long and Short Months of the Year). In the Japanese lunar calendar used until the Meiji period, a year was composed of synodic months designated "long" (30 days) and "short" (29 days) irregularly combined each year. The *Daishō no mai* was performed on the first day of the new year by a young male dancer chanting which months were long and which were short. Developed in the manner of Kabuki theater, the dance became one of the most popular in the repertoires of these dancers.[1]

Against the plain background, this young dancer strikes a pose with his right foot slightly raised. His gold *eboshi* (headdress) is decorated with stems of peony blossoms. In his right hand, covered by the sleeve, he holds a *gohei*, a Shinto ceremonial staff with cut paper strips; a sword completes his costume. The inscription (lower left) reads: *Edokoro Azukari Shō-goi-ge Tosa no Kami*

Fujiwara Mitsusada (Head of the Imperial Painting Office, in the Lower Fifth Rank, Tosa no Kami Fujiwara Mitsusada). The seal reads *Mitsusada no in* (the seal of Mitsusada).

In the early seventeenth century, independent artists known as *machieshi* (town painters, lacking the prestige of Kanō and Tosa school painters) took a keen interest in the recreation and amusements of the common people, depicting them vividly in large compositions on screens. Later in the seventeenth century, painters' interests shifted from general views to single figures, above all beautiful women and dancing young men. They were depicted on a plain ground in the smaller format of the hanging scroll. One reason for this change was that *machieshi* were catering to the popular demand of townsmen for relatively inexpensive paintings. Reflecting the painters' unimportant social status, these paintings rarely bear signature or seals.

Tosa Mitsusada was the second son of Tosa Tōmanmaru Mitsuyoshi (1700–1772). In 1754 Mitsusada became *Edokoro azukari* (Head of the Imperial Painting Office). The Tosa family originated in the early fifteenth century with Tosa Yukihiro, whose father Yukimitsu bore the name Fujiwara; thus, some Tosa painters used both names, as did Mitsusada in this painting.

The early Tosa painters were highly esteemed by aristocratic patrons; their position as court painters was inherited down to the nineteenth century. Their colorful decorative style changed little in that time. Their favorite themes were flowers and birds, illustrations of famous stories, such as the *Tale of Genji* and *Tales of Ise*, depicted in screens, narrative handscrolls, and fans. When imperial palace buildings were rebuilt or redecorated, the Tosa school artists painted these subjects on sliding screens. Mitsusada did sliding doors in the palace in the 1760s and again in 1789.[2]

This *wakashū* painting is significant because Mitsusada, the chief artist of the court, painted a subject of popular rather than courtly taste and, in addition, because the theme itself persisted from the late seventeenth to the early nineteenth century. Mitsusada's signature with his official title indicates that the painting was in fact produced for the imperial court or for an aristocrat.
— Y. W.

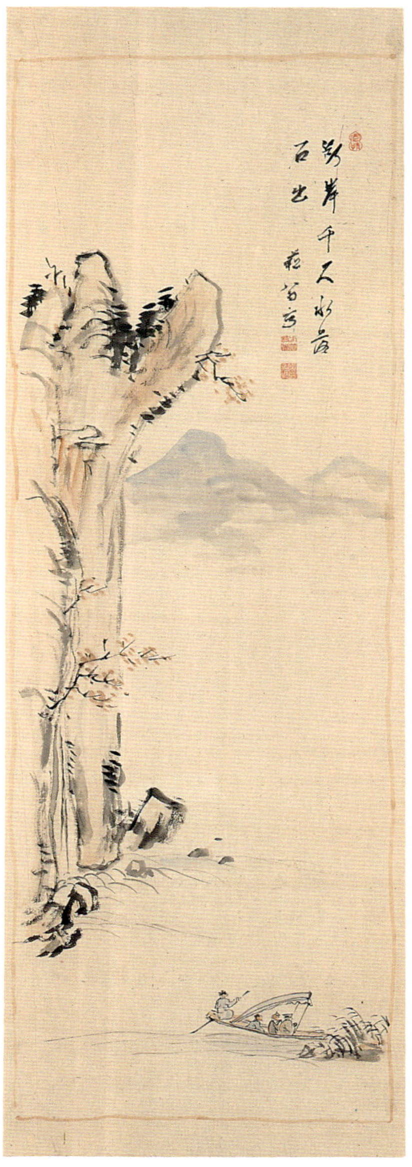

50. RED CLIFF

Nukina Kaioku (1778–1863)
Japan; Edo period, 19th century
Hanging scroll; ink and light color on paper
H: 120.6 cm (47½ in.) W: 41.0 cm (16⅛ in.)
1988.59.2
Gift of Mr. and Mrs. John B. Bunker

This scroll depicts the famous boat excursion of the Chinese scholar Su Shi (1036–1101) on the Yangzi River to the landmark known as the Red Cliff. From the cleft in the towering cliff a waterfall drops to the river, splashing the exposed rocks. The boat in the right foreground holds a boatman and three Chinese scholars seated under a canopy. Beyond the wide stretch of water are blue, distant mountains. A poem (upper right) is followed by the artist's signature *Suō sha* (painted by Suō) and two seals: *Hōchiku gisha* and *Kanboku seifuku*. A third seal, *Kijō*, is impressed at the beginning of the poem. Although the painting is not dated, Kaioku's *gō* (sobriquet), Suō, and two of the seals provide important clues to date it to 1850–1854, when the artist was in his seventies.[1] The poem is taken from the famous *Later Ode on Red Cliff* by Su Shi:

> Its sheer banks rising a thousand feet . . .
> The level of the water had fallen,
> Leaving boulders sticking out.[2]

Su Shi was a great poet and Confucian scholar of the Northern Song dynasty (960–1127). His *Earlier and Later Odes on the Red Cliff* describes boat excursions to this landmark, long a popular theme among Chinese literati painters. Educated in Chinese literature and poetry, Japanese literati (*bunjin*) painters of the Edo period (1615–1867) also favored it. Furthermore, they modeled their activities on the lives of Su Shi and other famous Chinese scholars and poets, frequently holding poetry parties, picnics, and boat excursions. The playful line in red-orange framing the picture indicates that it was the kind of impromptu work (*sekiga*, or party painting) done on social occasions.

Kaioku was a poet, *bunjin* painter, Confucian scholar, and one of the greatest calligraphers of the nineteenth century. He was born into a middle-ranking samurai family serving the daimyo of Tokushima, Awa Province, on the island of Shikoku. Generations of his family were archery instructors to the daimyo. Because of a weak constitution, Kaioku decided to become a scholar, and in 1810 or 1811 went to Osaka to attend the famous private school of Confucian study, Kaitokudō, where he later became an instructor and eventually its principal. However, he soon resigned and wandered around Mino, Kyoto, and Mount Kōya. In 1827, he settled in Kyoto and opened a private school, Shūseidō, where he taught Confucianism and later calligraphy and painting.

The economic and cultural enrichment of merchants and farmers in the second half of the Edo period produced Confucian scholars, teachers of all kinds, physicians, poets, writers, and above all *bunjin*. Through natural talent or special knowledge, they made a living outside the official class system of samurai, farmer, artisan, and merchant. Kaioku represents a typical *bunjin*. Since tuition from his students was an insufficient living, he sold his paintings and works of calligraphy to educated provincial merchant and farmer patrons. Often patrons and artists shared social occasions during which the artist sometimes composed poems and produced paintings depicting the event.[3] Kaioku very likely did this painting during or after he and his friends enjoyed a boat trip on the Yodogawa River that connects Osaka and Kyoto.
—Y. W.

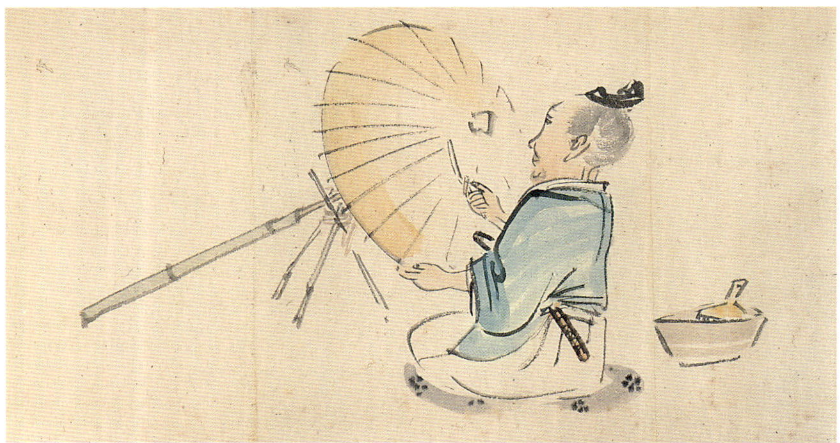

51. SKETCHES (DETAILS)

Shibata Zeshin (1807–1891)
Japan: late Edo to early Meiji period
Handscroll; ink and colors on paper
H: 29.8 cm (11¾ in.) W: 612.1 cm (241 in.)
87 D11
Gift of Mr. and Mrs. Willard G. Clark
and an anonymous donor

Shibata Zeshin was a painter and printmaker and is considered the greatest lacquer artist of the nineteenth century. In the West, he is one of the most renowned Japanese artists. The son of a sculptor in Edo (Tokyo), at age eleven he started his artistic career as a lacquer craftsman and apprenticed under Koma Kansai II (1766–1835), whose family had served the shogunate since 1636. At that time, lacquerers customarily depended on designer-painters to design their works. In 1822, realizing that he could in fact design his own works, Zeshin began painting lessons under Suzuki Nanrei (1775–1844) in Edo. Later he went to Kyoto to study under Okamoto Toyohiko (1773–1845), a famous Shijō school painter.

In this handscroll, Zeshin rapidly sketched a variety of independent themes.[1] The scroll is signed *Shibata Zeshin* and has two authentications by Zeshin's students, Yūshin and Chikushin.

Zeshin left many sketches, the earliest dating from his Kyoto period (1830s).[2] Like those in this handscroll, they reveal Zeshin's methodical pursuit of the direct study of nature and human figures in daily activities. Done in his typical fluid but well-controlled brushwork, the expression in this scroll is lively and cheerful. It illustrates Zeshin's talent in the medium as well as his debt to the Shijō school.

Despite his training in the Shijō school and having lived in Kyoto for some time, Zeshin's painting and lacquerware are the epitome of the merchant culture of Edo: his style is bold, his form simple, and his expression is light, cheerful, and witty.

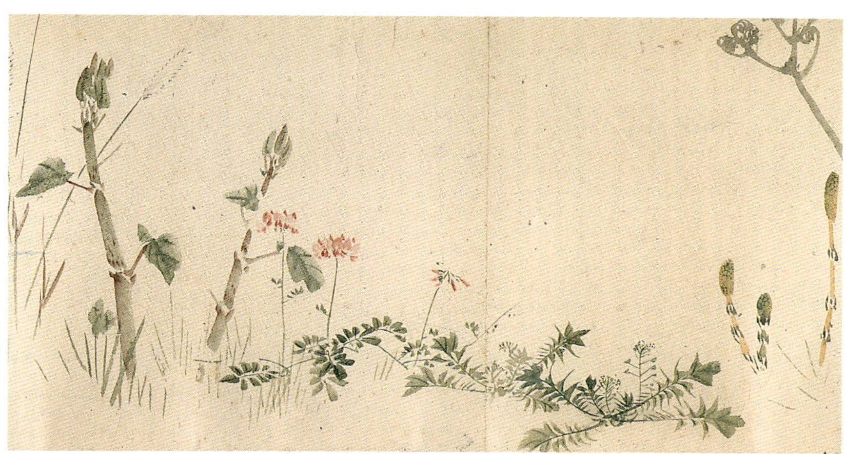

Zeshin lived before and after the Meiji Restoration of 1867, a violent period that transformed Japan from a feudal and isolated state into an imperial one whose emperor promoted contact with foreign countries. Western influence soon affected every facet of Japanese life, including artistic taste. Even the practice of art changed, as formal schooling replaced apprenticeship. In the Edo period, in which Zeshin attained artistic maturity, art had been commissioned by private patrons, and an artist's reputation spread slowly by word of mouth. In the new era, artists participated in competitions and exhibitions at home and abroad, and this exposure forever changed the nature of patronage in Japan.

Before 1867, Zeshin's patrons came from members of the affluent, leisured, and well-educated merchant society. For them he produced numerous ink paintings, lacquerware, and even a series of very large commissioned votive plaques (*ema*) that were offered at shrines by merchants' associations praying for business success.[3]

But after the Meiji Restoration of 1867, Zeshin's most important patronage came from the Imperial Household and the new administrative government, as well as from foreign buyers, an entirely new element in Japanese art patronage. Although initially reluctant to work for the Imperial Household, Zeshin, a proud *Edokko* (native son of Edo) soon found favor and accepted his new status.[4] His exhibited works were often purchased outright where they were shown (as was true for other artists of the period), sometimes by the emperor himself. Eventually Zeshin received imperial commissions of architectural scale.[5]

In 1890, Zeshin was appointed to the newly established Imperial Art Academy at an annual salary of 2500 yen (an enormous amount at the time) Further, he was paid additionally for commissioned pieces and received prize money or bonuses for outstanding works.[6]

The Meiji administrative government also actively encouraged artists to participate in international expositions. Zeshin was represented in expositions in Vienna (1873), Philadelphia (1876), and Paris (1889) and received

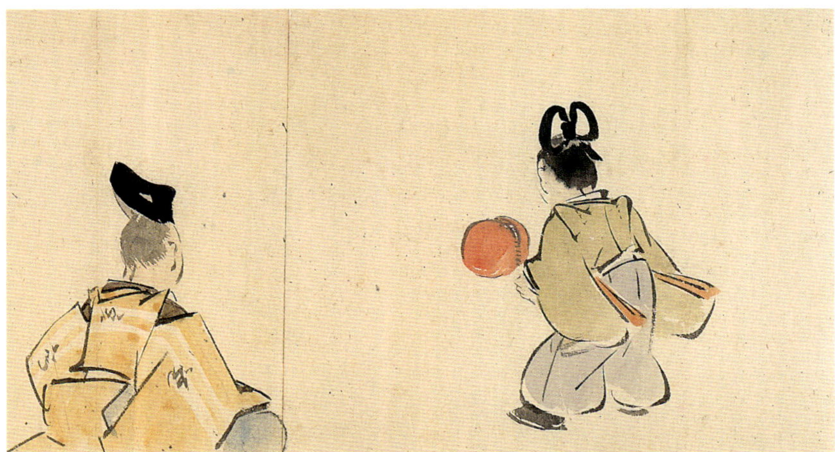

top honors; the government also gave him a monthly salary during his participation in these events.[7]

Japanese art attracted internationally active dealers and collectors; Zeshin's works were acquired by foreigners; prominent among them were two Americans, the poet and art scholar Ernest Fenollosa (1853–1908) and the collector William S. Bigelow (1850–1926), who both resided in Japan for extended periods.[8]

The influence of foreign taste adversely affected many Japanese artists, particularly lacquer craftsmen, who directed mediocre efforts to please the demand of an uncritical export market. But Shibata Zeshin survived this dynamic and extremely confusing period with his artistic integrity intact, maintaining the pride and self-discipline of a master. — Y. W.

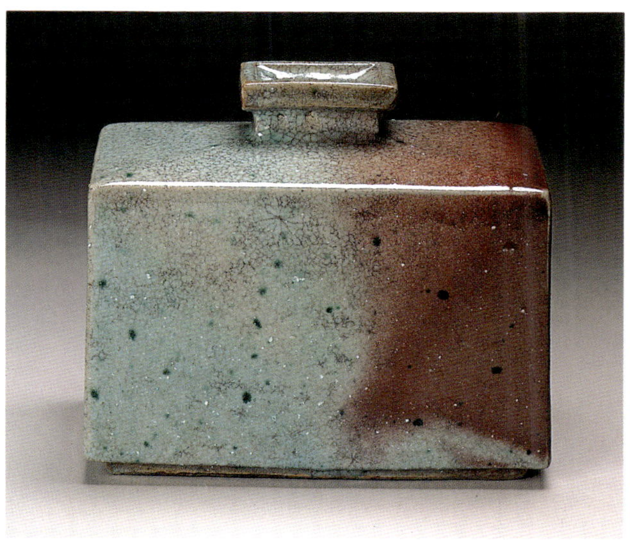

52. RECTANGULAR BOTTLE WITH COPPER OXIDE SPLASHES

Shōji Hamada (1894–1978)
Japan; Shōwa period
Glazed stoneware
H: 13.6 cm (5 3/8 in.) W: 16.6 cm (6 1/2 in.)
1988.36.2
Donated by Mr. and Mrs. L. H. Horiuchi in memory of Mrs. Lucy P. Gregg, who was an inspiration to all in the Horiuchi family

"It took me twenty years to unlearn what took me ten years to learn," the world-famous potter Shōji Hamada once said.[1] But in those ten hard-working years, Hamada gained the very practical skills of pottery-making as well as good teachers and friends. Following his early decision to become a first-class craftsman rather than a second-class fine artist, he spent from 1913 to 1916 in the Advanced Technical School of Tokyo and several more years in the Technical Research Institute in Kyoto. He learned wheel-throwing from another potter, Yūzō Kondō, and glaze making through thousands of test firings at the Institute, where he worked with another famous potter, Kanjirō Kawai, whom he met when he began to study in Tokyo in 1913.

Early in life Shōji Hamada's path also crossed those of several other gifted individuals. He held a deep respect for Hazan Itaya and Kenkichi Tomimoto, who inspired Hamada with their work as fine potters as well as their capacity for self-discipline. Above all, Hamada's meeting with and the deep respect he developed for Bernard Leach (1887–1979) and Sōetsu Yanagi (1889–1961) had a decisive influence on Hamada's becoming the leading figure of the very special and successful *mingei* craft movement that took place in Japan during the twentieth century.

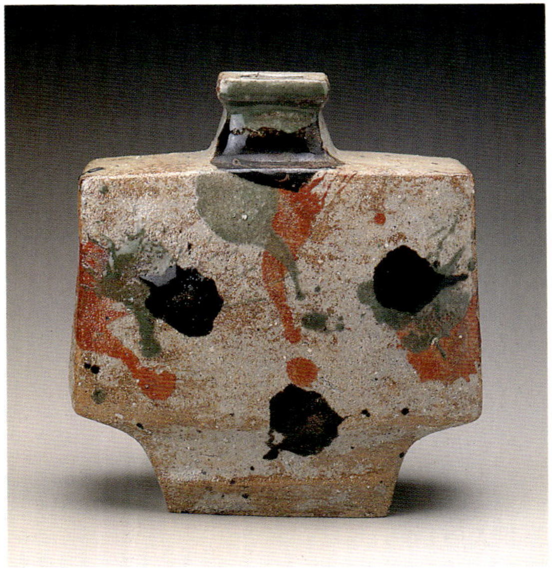

53. BOTTLE WITH SPLASHES OF GLAZES

Kanjirō Kawai (1890–1966)
Japan; Shōwa period, 1960s
Glazed stoneware
H: 21.5 cm (8½ in.) W: 19.6 cm (7¾ in.)
1988.58.2
Gift of Miss Yoshiko Uchida

The unique artistic and intellectual collaboration that inspired these men produced unique and far-reaching results. Hamada, who admired Leach's work, came in 1919 to help him at his new and relocated kiln in Tokyo, after Leach's first studio in Yanagi's residence burned. From this relationship came Hamada's residency in England. Accepting Leach's request to accompany him to England to help build a Japanese-style kiln, Hamada left his position and Japan. From 1920 to 1923, he and Leach devoted themselves to utilitarian pottery production in the Cornish village of St. Ives. There Hamada developed the strong conviction that living in an unspoiled rural community enables one to make good, unaffected ceramics. This conviction later led him to settle in Mashiko, a small village a little north of Tokyo where farmer-potters produced wares for the local market using an ordinary and rather inferior clay.

Settling in Mashiko was not simple. It was a small exclusive community, typical of so rural an area, where newcomers were regarded not only as outsiders but often as evil, for long periods of time.[2] Hamada, now married, spent several winter months in Okinawa, away from the discrimination and poverty in Mashiko, to survive and learn another unspoiled way of life as well as traditional Okinawan pottery-making.

In 1923 Hamada returned to Japan with examples of English slipware that made a deep impression on Sōetsu Yanagi, who had been promoting Korean ceramics by unknown craftsmen. In 1921 he declared his intention to establish a museum in Korea devoted to such crafts and opened it in 1924 in Seoul.

Through Hamada, Kawai, already a successful potter excelling in Chinese-style fine ceramics, met Yanagi. Yanagi's sincerity and his growing collection of previously neglected works by nameless craftsmen and sculptures by the wandering monk Mokujiki (1718–1810) so impressed Kawai that he joined Yanagi's movement. All three men went on search-and-collect journeys to China, Korea, and remote areas in Japan. Yanagi records Kawai's childlike openness and excitement at finding good wares in small shops and sometimes even in villagers' warehouses, long forgotten and gathering dust.

In late 1925, during one of those trips, Yanagi, Kawai, and Hamada directed their intense discussions on the beauty of what had been simply called *getemono* (low-class ware), *zakki* (miscellaneous ware), and *aramono* (rough ware) into an organized effort to promote "crafts for people," *minshū-teki kōgei* (from which the term *mingei* was coined). They decided to found a museum devoted to collecting and showing such objects. The first volume of *Kōgei*, the periodical devoted to the movement, was published in 1931. In 1936 the Nippon Mingei-kan Museum was opened in Tokyo.

Kawai, who already had three extremely successful one-man shows in Tokyo, was ready to abandon fine ware and assured success as a studio potter in order to produce the kind of ware Yanagi was advocating. In his early career Kawai had been fortunate in having understanding patrons and a popular following for his fine ceramics. When he later began to search for a simple style in the spirit of Yanagi's *mingei* movement, Kawai again received the warm support of a broad spectrum of patrons with academic, business, and social connections.[3] A very fine writer from his youth and a man of high intelligence and poetic sensibility, he undertook through lectures and publications to enlighten those beyond his immediate followers.

Both Hamada and Kawai concentrated on their own creative works but also traveled far and wide to work with potters in remote villages, encouraging them to preserve old traditions threatened by encroaching modernization. They also helped craftsmen by providing outlets for pottery as well as other crafts—weaving, wood objects, and handmade papers. Their influence reached potters in Europe and the United States.

On this characteristically unsigned bottle, Hamada used only copper oxide to create a simple but strong work.[4] On his bottle, Kawai splashed different glazes with three bright contrasting colors. Yet both potters' works, simple in form and technique, are visually striking. The Hamada bottle seems to be an early one, while Kawai's is from the 1960s, when he made a series of works with the same three colors of glazes.[5]—Y.K.

NOTES

Cat. no. 1

1. Alessio Bombaci, *The Kufic Inscription in Persian Verses in the Court of the Royal Palace of Mas'ud III at Ghazni (ISMEO Reports and Memoirs)*, vol. 5 (Rome: Istituto Italiano per il Medio ed Estremo Oriente, 1966). The first publication of part of this dado was by Samuel Flury, "Le décor épigraphique des monuments de Ghazna," *Syria* 6 (1925), pp. 61–90. Bombaci illustrates part of this panel, fig. 124 in pl. 30, showing only the inscription.

2. The most plausible reading of the text on this panel is: *[amir-i(?)] shahid yak chandi ...* (the martyred [Amir] for a while ...), probably referring to an earlier martyred Ghaznavid sultan. David Monchi-Zadeh, "Notes on the Kufic Inscription of the Royal Palace of Mas'ud III at Ghazni," *Orientalia Suecana* 16 (1967) [1968], pp. 113–25.

Cat. no. 2

1. The other known example is a miniature painting from the collection of Bharat Kala Bhavan, Varanasi; see B. N. Goswamy, *Essence of Indian Art* (San Francisco: Asian Art Museum, 1986), no. 118.

2. Amy G. Poster, *From Indian Earth, 4,000 Years of Terracotta Art* (New York: The Brooklyn Museum, 1986), no. 94.

Cat. no. 3

Published: Ulrich von Schroeder, *Indo-Tibetan Bronzes* (Hong Kong: Visual Dharma Publications, 1981), pl. 21B.

1. Pratapaditya Pal, *Bronzes of Kashmir* (Graz, Austria: Akademische Druck -u. Verlagsanstalt, 1975), p. 22.

2. Three other metal images in the Asian Art Museum collection, a Padmapani, an eleven-headed Avalokiteshvarȧ from Ladakh, and a Bonpo image from Western Tibet, are all later manifestations of the Kashmiri style. (60 S230, 60 S231, and 84 B1).

3. Pal, *Bronzes of Kashmir*, p. 9. See also Douglas Barrett, "Bronzes of Northwest India and Western Pakistan," *Lalit Kala* 11 (1962).

Cat. no. 4

1. Other pages from the same Qur'an are found in the Museum Rietberg in Zurich, Chester Beatty Library in Dublin, Cincinnati Art Museum, Rhode Island School of Design, Fogg Art Museum of Harvard University, Los Angeles County Museum of Art, and various private collections. The complete manuscript was previously held by M. Riefstahl. The bulk of it is now split between Stuart Cary Welch and the late Philip Hofer, from whose former collection this leaf comes.

Cat. no. 5

1. Robert Skelton, "Collecting Indian Miniatures," in Daniel J. Ehnbom, *Indian Miniatures, The Ehrenfeld Collection* (New York: Hudson Hills Press in association with the American Federation of Arts, 1985), pp. 11–12.

2. For two more pages from the same album, see P. & D. Colnaghi & Co. Ltd., *Paintings from Mughal India* (London: Lund Humphries, 1979), pls. 21 and 40.

Cat. no. 6

Published: Daniel J. Ehnbom, *Indian Miniatures, The Ehrenfeld Collection* (New York: Hudson Hills Press in association with the American Federation of Arts, 1985), p. 156, no. 72.

1. Stuart Cary Welch, *Indian Drawings and Painted Sketches, Sixteenth through Nineteenth Centuries* (New York: Asia Society, 1976), p. 85.

Cat. no. 7

1. Karl Khandalavala, *Kishangarh Painting* (India: Lalit Kala Akademi, n.d.).

2. There are conflicting opinions on this theory; see Eric Dickinson and Karl Khandalavala, *Kishangarh Painting* (India: Lalit Kala Akademi, 1959), and Faiyaz Ali Khan, "Kishangarh Painting," *Roopa-Lekha*, vol.40: 1–2, pp. 83–87.

3. M. S. Randhawa and J. K. Galbraith, *Indian Painting* (Boston: Houghton Mifflin, 1968).

Cat. no. 8

1. For more information on the Daniells, see Mildred Archer, *Early Views of India, The Picturesque Journeys of Thomas and William Daniell 1786–1794* (London: Thames and Hudson, 1980).

Cat. no. 9

1. Mildred Archer, *Company Drawings in the India Office Library* (London: Her Majesty's Stationery Office, 1972), p. 1.

2. Mildred Archer, *Natural History Drawings in the India Office Library* (London: Her Majesty's Stationery Office, 1962), p. 54.

3. Identifications and current nomenclature provided by Stephen F. Bailey, Dept. of Ornithology and Mammalogy, California Academy of Sciences.

Cat nos. 10, 11

1. For more information on Bidri ware, see Susan Stronge, *Bidri Ware, Inlaid Metalwork from India* (London: Victoria and Albert Museum, 1985). The only Bidri piece comparable to this example is the silver inlaid *huqqa* base from the National Museum, New Delhi, which is decorated with scenes depicting passages from the *Padmavati*, a romance between Padmavati, a princess of Ceylon, and Ratansen, king of Chitor. See Krishna Lal, "A Unique *Huqqa*-base in the National Museum of India Depicting the *Padmavat* of Jayasi," *Facets of Indian Art* (London: Victoria and Albert Museum, 1986), pp. 260–64.

Cat. no. 12

1. For a discussion of these textiles, see Mattiebelle Gittinger, *Master Dyers to the World; Technique and Trade in Early Indian Dyed Cotton Textiles* (Washington, D.C.: The Textile Museum, 1982), pp. 155–66.

2. *The Voyage of François Pyrard of Laval*, trans. A. Gray, vol. 2 (London: Hakluyt Society, 1887–1889), p. 247.

3. The usefulness of this dating technique may vary from area to area; different workshops may have favored different techniques.

Cat. no. 13

1. Pratapaditya Pal and Julia Meech-Pekarik, *Buddhist Book Illuminations* (New Delhi and New York: Ravi Kumar, 1988), p. 95.

2. Ibid., p. 105, pl. 26.

Cat. no. 14

1. Zhu Jiajin, "Gugong suozang mingqing liangdai youguan xizang di wenwu" (Cultural objects related to Tibet of the Ming and Qing dynasties in the Palace Museum Collection), *Wenwu* 7 (1959), pp. 14–19.

Cat. no. 15

1. Another name for Yongs-'dzin Ngag-dbang bzang-po was Bde-chen chos-'khor yongs-'dzin. He was the fourth 'Brug-chen incarnate, and abbot of the Bde-chen chos-'khor monastery belonging to the 'Brug-pa bKa'-brgyud-pa, a subsect of the Kagyu-pa. I thank Dan Martin of Bloomington, Indiana, for this information.

2. See Detlef Ingo Lauf, *Tibetan Sacred Art, The Heritage Of Tantra* (Berkeley and London: Shambhala, 1976), no. 79, for another bronze image of Ngag-dbang bzang-po. He wears identical headgear, and Lauf describes it as a hermit lama's cap.

Cat. nos. 17, 18

1. Claudius C. Muller and Walter Raunig, *Der Weg zum Dach der Welt* (Austria: Pinguin-Verlag, 1983?), p. 244.

2. Arthur Leeper, personal communication.

3. Valrae Reynolds, personal communication. For more information on the *gya-lu che* costume, see her article, "From a Lost World: Tibetan Costumes and Textiles," *Orientations* (March, 1981), pp. 6–22.

4. Spencer Chapman, *Lhasa, The Holy City* (London: Readers Union, 1940), p. 219.

5. Another example, complete with a small medallion, was auctioned by Sotheby; see *Indian, Himalayan, South-east Asian Art, and Indian Miniatures* (New York: Sept. 20–21, 1985), no. 520.

6. Chapman, *Lhasa*: "Leaders of above dance, and youthful trumpeters," photograph between pp. 272–73; Rosemary Jones Tung, *A Portrait of Lost Tibet* (New York: Holt, Rinehart and Winston, 1980), pls. 41 and 97.

Cat. no. 19

1. Dr. Badrul Akram, Director of Provincial Museums, Java, has suggested the facial features of this Buddha are similar to sculptures from the region of Tegal (personal communication). For a sculpture of a Tara from Wonosobo (near Tegal in Northern Java), seated on a comparable throne with a flame-encircled aureole, see *Borobudur* (Brussels: Palais des Beaux-Arts, 1977), pl. 58.

2. See A. J. Bernet Kempers, *Ancient Indonesian Art*, (Cambridge, Mass.: Harvard University Press, 1959), pls. 60, 62, 63, and Pauline Lunsingh Scheurleer and Marijke J. Klokke, *Ancient Indonesian Bronzes* (Amsterdam: Rijksmuseum, and Leiden: E. J. Brill, 1988), pl. 57 and pp. 19–20, for a discussion of this type of Buddha.

3. For comparison, see *Borobudur*, 1977, pl. 58 and p. 148, and Bernet Kempers, *Ancient Indonesian Art*, pls. 60, 62, 63.

4. For comparison, see the clothing of the Avalokiteshvara and Vasudhara (cat. no. 20) and Scheurleer and Klokke, pl. 38.

Cat. no. 20

1. Pratapaditya Pal, *The Sensuous Immortals* (Los Angeles: Los Angeles County Museum of Art, 1977), pl. 116. Pauline Lunsingh Scheurleer and Marijke J. Klokke, *Ancient Indonesian Bronzes* (Amsterdam: Rijksmuseum, and Leiden: E. J. Brill, 1988), pls. 27, 41, and 53.

2. There is a small silver image of Manjusri so similar in style and size (5.8 cm) that it may be from the same group; see J. E. van L'ouhuizen-de Leeuw, *Indo-Javanese Metalwork* (Stuttgart: Linden-Museum, 1984). See also the group recently sold at auction, Christie's Amsterdam, *Fine Indonesian Sculpture and Works of Art* (Amsterdam: June, 1989), lots 279–282, cover and pl. p. 76.

Cat. no. 21

1. Susan Rodgers, *Power and Gold; Jewelry from Indonesia, Malaysia, and the Philippines* (Geneva: Barbier-Muller Museum, 1985).

2. John N. Miksic, *Small Finds: Ancient Javanese Gold* (Singapore: National Museum, 1988), pp. 3–4.

3. Himansu Bhusan Sarkar, *Corpus of the Inscriptions of Java* (Calcutta: Firma K. L. Mukhopadhyay, 1971), I:20.

4. For examples, see Sarkar, *Corpus of the Inscriptions of Java*, I:71, 283, and 284; II:2, 17, and 31.

5. F. D. K. Bosch, "Gouden vingerringen uit de Hindoe-Javaansche tijdperk," *Djawa* 7 (1927), pp. 305–20. A more recent discussion can be found in Miksic, *Small Finds*, pp. 13–15.

6. See A. J. Bernet Kempers, *Ancient Indonesian Art* (Cambridge, Mass.: Harvard University Press, 1959), pl. 319, and Miksic, *Small Finds*, pl. 42, for comparable examples.

7. See Miksic, *Small Finds*, pls. 14–20, for similar objects. He calls these pieces rod finials.

8. See Miksic, *Small Finds*, pls. 20, 29, and Bernet Kempers, *Ancient Indonesian Art*, pl. 319, for similar examples.

9. For similar examples, see Miksic, *Small Finds*, pls. 7–9.

10. Bernet Kempers, *Ancient Indonesian Art*, pls. 41, 84, 158, 172–76, 181, and 217. An additional example is in Claire Holt, *Art in Indonesia* (Ithaca: Cornell University Press, 1967), pl. 40.

11. This practice is still followed in India and in Southeast Asia, and evidence exists from the tenth century in Vietnam that sculptures were decorated. See *Art and Archaeology of Vietnam: Asian Crossroad of Cultures* (Washington, D.C.: Smithsonian Institution, 1961). The bodhisattvas found in Bernet Kempers, *Ancient Indonesian Art*, pls. 172–76, are an example of images with distended earlobes devoid of jewelry.

12. See Bernet Kempers, *Ancient Indonesian Art*, pls. 192 and 208.

13. Miksic, *Small Finds*, pl. 50 and p. 17.

Cat. no. 22

1. Urs Ramseyer, *The Art and Culture of Bali* (Oxford: Oxford University Press, 1977), pls. 40 and 44; A. J. Bernet Kempers, *Monumental Bali* (The Hague: Van Goor Sonen Den Haag, n.d.), pls. 42–43.

2. Bernet Kempers, *Monumental Bali*, pp. 173–74.

3. R. Goris, "The Position of the Blacksmiths," *Bali: Studies in Life, Thought, and Ritual*, Selected Studies on Indonesia by Dutch Scholars, 5 (The Hague and Bandung: W. van Hoeve, 1960), pp. 290–99.

4. Bernet Kempers, *Monumental Bali*, pp. 118–19.

Cat. no. 23

1. Urs Ramseyer, *The Art and Culture of Bali* (Oxford: Oxford University Press, 1977), pls. 40 and 44. A. J. Bernet Kempers, *Ancient Indonesian Art* (Cambridge, Mass.: Harvard University Press, 1959), pls. 247, 248, 265, and 339a.

2. Robert W. Hefner, *Hindu Javanese: Tengger Tradition and Islam* (New York: Princeton University Press, 1985); see especially pp. 58, 67, 70, and 120.

3. Hefner, *Hindu Javanese*, p. 44.

Cat. no. 24

1. See the early Indian Varaha figures from Eran, Udayagiri, and Aphsad.

2. Kamaleswar Bhattacharya, *Les Religions Brahmaniques dans l'ancien Cambodge* (Paris: Publication de l'École Française d'Extrême Orient, 1961), vol. XLIX, p. 168.

3. *Bhagavata Purana*, vol. 8, part II, p. 749.

4. Frederick M. Asher, *The Art of Eastern India, 300–800* (Minneapolis: University of Minnesota Press, 1980), pp. 54–55 and pls. 91–94.

5. Vettam Mani, *Puranic Encyclopaedia* (Delhi: Motilal Banarsidass, 1975), p. 770.

Cat. no. 25

1. See Sherman E. Lee, *Ancient Cambodian Sculpture* (New York: The Asia Society, 1969), pl. 56, for an example of a finial with dancing figures. A very similar example of bronze dancing *apsaras* is in the Bangkok National Museum.

Cat. no. 26

1. Translated by Nai Pan Hla by communication with Donald M. Stadtner, University of Texas, Austin, 1989.

2. *Archaeological Survey of India: Burma Circle* (Office of the Superintendent, Government Printing Office, Burma, 1913/14–1914/15), pp. 11–16, pl. 5.

3. See Donald M. Stadtner, "We Women Will Catch Him Like a Bird in the Net of Concupiscence," *The Society for Asian Art Newsletter* 2:28 (Winter 1989), p. 6.

Cat. no. 27

1. Temple vases of this kind have been little noticed or studied but constitute a significant series of ceramics made during a time of wavering Chinese influence in northern Vietnam. This example and all its counterparts have traditionally been attributed to the

Bat Trang kilns, approximately 100 kilometers northwest of present-day Hanoi. Whole or fragmentary examples of this series may still be seen on offering altars of older temples near Hanoi. Other vessels from this series are now in Hanoi's National Museum of History, the Tokugawa Art Museum, the Tokyo National Museum, and the Musée Guimet, Paris.

Cat no. 28

1. Fred H. Andrews, *Wall Paintings from Ancient Shrines in Central Asia, Recovered by Sir Aurel Stein, K.C.I.E.* (London: Oxford University Press, 1948), pls. XVI–XVIII, XXVII.

2. See, for example, Roderick Whitfield, *The Art of Central Asia, The Stein Collection in the British Museum,* vol. 3 (Tokyo: Kodansha and the Trustees of the British Museum, 1982), pls. 71–72; for examples from Kizil, see Herbert Härtel, Marianne Yaldiz, et al., *Along the Ancient Silk Routes, Central Asian Art from the West Berlin State Museums* (New York: The Metropolitan Museum of Art, 1982), pls. 39–40.

3. Giuseppe Tucci, *Transhimalaya* (Geneva: Nagel Publishers, 1973), p. 112; from the Bonardi Collection.

4. See Luc Kwanten, *Imperial Nomads, A History of Central Asia, 500–1500* (Leicester: Leicester University Press, 1979); Elisabeth Pinks, *Die Uiguren von Kan-chou in der frühen Sung-Zeit (960–1028)* (Wiesbaden: Otto Harrassowitz, 1968).

Cat. no. 29

1. James Cahill, *An Index of Early Chinese Painters and Paintings, T'ang, Sung, and Yuan* (Berkeley: University of California Press, 1980), p. 298, and Howard Rogers, unpublished manuscript on Lai'an.

Cat. no. 30

1. *Shanghai gudai lishi wenwu tulu* (Catalogue of ancient historical relics from Shanghai) (Shanghai: Shanghai Educational Press, 1981), pp. 50–51.

2. *Suzhou Huqiuta chutu wenwu* (Relics unearthed at the Huqiu pagoda, Suzhou) (Beijing: Cultural Press, 1958), p. 24.

3. A biography appears in *Mochizuki Bukkyo Daijiten,* vol. 4 (Tokyo: Sekai Seitan Kankō Kyōkai, 1961–1967), p. 3148.

Cat. no. 31

1. For a thorough study of Wang Hui's relationship to Zhou Lianggong, see Hongnam Kim, "Chou Liang-kung and his *Tu-hua-lu* (Lives of Painters): Patron, Critic and Painters in Seventeenth Century China" (Ph.D. dissertation, Yale University, 1985).

2. Li Yufen, ed., *Yanke tiba* or *Wang Fengchang shuhua tiba* (Colophons on Calligraphy and paintings by Wang Shimin) (n.p.: Tongzhou Lishi Ouboluoshi, 1910), ch. *xia,* pp. 8–9.

Cat. no. 32

1. Ferdinand Lessing, *Yung-ho-kung, An Iconography of the Lamaist Cathedral in Peking, with Notes on Lamaist Mythology and Cult* (Stockholm-Goteborg: Elanders boktryckeri aktiebolog, 1942).

2. See Harold Kahn, *Monarchy in the Emperor's Eyes, Image and Reality in the Ch'ien-lung Reign* (Cambridge, Mass.: Harvard University Press, 1971), pp. 182, 185.

3. Walter Eugene Clark, *Two Lamaist Pantheons* (Cambridge, Mass.: Harvard University Press, 1937).

4. *Xizang Tangka* (Tibetan thangkas) (Beijing: Cultural Press, 1985), pl. 97. The size is given as 235 × 83 cm, a format similar to the Asian Art Museum scroll, which has been cut down slightly at top and bottom.

5. *Kuo-li Ku-kung Bo-wu-yuan Tz'u-hsiu* (Embroideries in the National Palace Museum) (Tokyo: Gakken and the National Palace Museum, Taipei, 1970), pl. 46. The size here is 211 × 86.5 cm, very close to the present piece at 209.5 × 86 cm.

6. *Xizang Tangka,* p. 190.

7. *Pi-tien Chu-lin* with *Hsü-pien* (Supplement) and *San-pien* (Taipei: National Palace Museum, 1971), vol. 10, p. 23.

Cat. no. 33

1. Hugh Moss, *By Imperial Command; An Introduction to Ch'ing Imperial Painted Enamels* (Hong Kong: Hibiya, 1976).

Cat. no. 34

1. During the Yongzheng reign, the glass studio was moved to the Summer Palace.

2. This technique demonstrates the Qing glassmaker's early mastery in shaping a vessel whose walls are "clear, thin and brittle," characteristics mentioned in texts that define products of the Cantonese glassmakers.

3. Not even the Palace Museum, Beijing, which holds the world's largest assemblage of Yongzheng-marked glass (twelve pieces), has such a piece. The only known nearly identical specimens are two engraved bowls with covers that have been in the Victoria and Albert Museum, London, since 1833, when they were purchased by the legendary Chinese art curator Stephen Bushell. A four-character imperial mark (*Yongzheng nian zhi*) is precisely incised in a single horizontal line just below the rim of this bowl. The two dynastic characters *Da Qing* (Great Qing), customarily found in conjunction with reign marks on the other imperially sanctioned applied arts of the time, are wholly absent on this example and nearly all other imperial glass made during the early Qing. The shortened dynastic-reign mark might be due to its having been established by edict when the Kangxi emperor created the imperial glasshouse. Certainly the most relevant and only surviving glass object with a Kangxi regnal mark attests to such an early appearance of only four characters (*Kangxi Yu zhi*). The location of the regnal mark on this example, just below the rim, has precedents in Ming fifteenth-century porcelain conventions.

4. Crizzling takes several different forms—scaling, fine crazing, a sour-smelling liquid-like film, surface iridescence with pitting, and silvery pitting.

5. As early as 1937, the late William B. Honey, a British specialist, observed and wrote about common traits of the manufacture and condition of Chinese and European glass in the late seventeenth and early eighteenth centuries. He hypothesized a foundation for probable time and place of origin. He noted that all glass displayed crizzling to some degree, an observation now correctly recognized as a chemical phenomenon but one which, when first introduced, was deemed "heretical."

Cat. nos. 35–37

1. John E. Vollmer, *Decoding Dragons, Status Garments in Ch'ing Dynasty China* (Eugene, Oregon: University of Oregon Museum of Art, 1983); Verity Wilson, *Chinese Dress* (London: Victoria and Albert Museum, 1986).

2. Schuyler Cammann, "The Development of the Mandarin Square," *Harvard Journal of Asiatic Studies* 8:2 (August, 1944), pp. 71–130.

3. Irene Emery, *The Primary Structure of Fabrics* (Washington, D.C.: The Textile Museum, 1980), pp. 133–36.

Cat. no. 38

1. The seven other wheeled carts are in the following collections: Mr. and Mrs. Dale Keller, Honolulu; Mrs. Gregory Henderson, Boston, Mass.; Horim Art Museum, Seoul; National Museum of Korea, Seoul (two vessels); Tokyo National Museum, Tokyo; and Ewha Women's University Museum, Seoul.

2. *T'oqi* (Pottery), *Hanguk ui Mi* series, vol. 5 (Seoul: Chungang Ilbosa, 1981), p. 156.

Cat. no. 40

1. The translation is by Dr. Kumja Kim. The term *Ch'amp'an* is a rank title equivalent to the Second Minister of one of the government boards. The boards that had this position during the Chosŏn period were War, Works, Taxation, Rites, Punishments, and Personnel. See Edward Wilett Wagner, "List of Government Offices and Posts, with Indication of Rank (in Yi Korea)," *The Literati Purges: Political Conflict in Early Yi Korea* (Cambridge, Mass.: Harvard University Press, 1974), Appendix A, pp. 128–33.

Cat. no. 41

1. Shōichi Narazaki, *Shirashi, Nippon Tōji Zenshū*, vol. 6 (Tokyo: Chūōkōronsha, 1976), p. 46.

2. The foot appears to have been thrown onto the body, a widely used technique in which, after the body is leather-hard (firm to the touch but still malleable), the additional coil of clay is added to form a foot, and the whole piece is then thrown on the wheel to give a final shape. A hairline crack exists at the joint, suggesting this difference in dryness between the body and the foot when they were joined. Ibid., p. 47.

3. Many other examples of ash-glazed ware from Sanage kilns have been excavated from the Heijō capital (710–794) site in Nara. Some were accompanied by written documents on wooden slabs dated Tempyō-hōu (757–764), indicating that this type of ware emerged no later than the mid-eighth century. Ibid., pl. 37.

4. While it is not known where this piece was found, a comparative study eliminates other kilns and places as sites of fabrication and confirms its manufacture at the Sanage complex, most probably within the Kurozasa area of that complex. In fact, a pitcher of nearly the same shape and dimensions was excavated from Kurozasa Kiln No. 7, datable to the first half of the ninth century.

5. Ash-glazed ware was made in other provinces in the Tōkai district in Central Japan, in Mikawa, Tōtōmi, Mino, and Ise; however, those from the Sanage kilns were the most numerous.

Cat. no. 42

1. A Muqi monkey painting is in Daitokuji. A pair of monkey screens attributed to Sesshū is in the Museum of Fine Arts, Boston.

2. For example, the artist's seal was misdeciphered as *Ryūkyō*, and he had been so known. The most recent research on Shikibu is by Yūji Yamashita, "Shikibu Terutada no kenkyū—Kantō suibokuga ni kansuru ichikōsatsu" (A study of Shikibu Terutada: An observation on ink painting in the Kantō area), *Kokka* 1084 (1985), pp. 11–31.

3. The complete fan screens can be seen in Yamashita, fig. 3. The Denver Art Museum has two fan paintings from this pair of fan screens.

4. Ōsen Keisan, *Ho'an keikashū* (1485), p. 593. Tanaka Kisaku, "Senmen chirashi byōbu ni tsuite" (On the screen decorated with pictures in the shape of a fan), *Bijutsu kenkyū* 51 (1936), p. 93.

5. Nobuo Tsuji, "Kano Motonobu" (II), *Bijutsu kenkyū* 249 (1966), p. 8.

6. Yamashita, "Shikibu Terutada," pp. 19–23.

7. Ibid., pp. 23–27 and fig. 22.

8. For Shikibu's *Dharma* painting, see ibid., fig. 22.

Cat nos. 43–45

1. A standard recording of *chanoyu* gatherings lists names of the guests, utensils used, and the *kaiseki* menu. Such records are useful references for historians in many fields.

2. The basic number of utensils used to hold a *chanoyu* gathering is no fewer than fifty for a simple *usucha* (thin tea) service.

3. Remaining pairs of filled holes along the crack indicate that the original repair used metal staples.

4. Ryōichi Fujioka, *Oribe, Tōji Taikei,* vol. 12 (Tokyo: Heibonsha, 1978), pp. 95–96.

Cat. no. 46

1. Monju is also called Bunshu, since his name in Chinese characters could be read more than one way.

2. This reference enables the letter to be dated 1632.

3. Isao Kumakura, *Go-Mizunoo Tennō* (Tokyo: Asahi Shimbun, 1982), p. 277.

4. Go-Mizunoo's many *waka* poems convey his inner turmoil at this enforced mandate and his conflicts with the shogunate's policies. After his early and sudden abdication, in

defiance of the shogunate's continuing aggression, Go-Mizunoo culminated his artistic endeavors in the construction of a complex of country tea houses and the ambitious landscaping of the surrounding hillside garden, of what is now known as the Shūgakuin detached palace.

Cat. no. 47

1. In order, they are: 12, 20, 22, 25, 26, 29, 30, 31, 21, 48, 49, and 53. Chapter 21 is erroneously placed here with the title for Chapter 45, "Hashihime." Nothing is known of the location or survival of the other chapters. It is safe to assume that the set was once complete, since all other examples in similar format are assumed to have been composed of complete sets. From the box and an empty album that accompany this scroll, we know that the panels, formerly mounted in this album, were recomposed as a scroll sometime after 1695, the date inscribed on the box.

2. *Kana*, a set of Japanese syllabaries, was an extremely simplified cursive script developed from the so-called Chinese grass script and was considered women's handwriting.

3. Now in the Gotō Art Museum Collection and Tokugawa Reimeikan Collection, both in Tokyo; published in Ivan Morris, *Genji Monogatari* (Tokyo: Kodansha International, 1971).

4. Yōichi Katagiri, ed., and Osaka Joshidaigaku Monogatari Kenkyūkai, *Genji Monogatari Ekotoba* (Kyoto: Daigakudō Shoten, 1983).

Cat. no. 48

1. Aimi Kōu, "Fukae Roshū no funbo hakken o megutte" (Of the discovery of Fukae Roshū's grave), *Yamato Bunka* 31 (October, 1959), pp. 16–29.

2. Ibid., p. 24. Roshū made two more versions of this subject, a six-panel screen at the Cleveland Museum of Art, and another at the Umezawa Kinenkan Museum, Tokyo.

3. Itō Toshiko, *Ise monogatari-e* (Tokyo: Kadokawa Shoten, 1984), p. 24.

Cat. no. 49

1. Nobuo Tsuji, "Kanbun bijin kara Moronobu e" (Development of beauty paintings in Kanbun era to Moronobu's beauty), in *Genshoku Nihon no bijutsu*, vol. 24, *Fūzokuga to ukiyoe* (Tokyo: Shōgakukan, 1971), p. 159. Some scholars believe this type of dancing figure is performing the Dance of Narihara; see *Kinsei fūzokuzufu*, vol. 10, *Kabuki* (Tokyo: Shōgakukan, 1983), p. 78.

2. The Edokoro masters apparently had a studio outside of but adjacent to the palace, where they could mobilize artisans and assistants for large-scale projects. For example, Tosa Mitsuoki had his studio in Teramachi Marutamachi; see Yoshida Tomoyuki, "Kinsei Tosa-ha, Mitsunori kara Mitsuoki e" (Tosa School in Pre-modern Period: from Mitsunori to Mitsuoki), *Kobijutsu* 71 (July, 1984), p. 74.

Cat. no. 50

1. Kaioku began to use the name Suō around 1850. The seal *Kanboku seifuku* first appeared in his works in 1850 and was used until his death; the seal *Kijō* appeared in 1841 and was used until 1854. See Masanobu Hosono, "Nukina Suō shōron" (A study on Nukina Kaioku), *Museum* 290 (May, 1975), p. 4.

2. The second line in Su Shi's ode, "The mountains were very high, the moon looks small," is omitted by Kaioku. Su Shi's odes were translated by B. Watson in *The Red Cliff* (Taipei: National Palace Museum, 1984).

3. Yoko Woodson, "Traveling Bunjin Painters and Their Patrons: Economic Life Style and Art of Rai San'yō and Tanomura Chikuden" (Ph.D. dissertation, University of California, Berkeley, 1983).

Cat. no. 51

1. The subjects of this handscroll are: an umbrella maker, spring plants, a frog and a rabbit, a ceramic bowl, morning-glory blossoms, a writing box, rocks and plants in a bowl, a wind chime, a bunch of grapes, a young courtier taking a *kemari* (a sort of kick-ball) lesson, four people at a poetry gathering, a priest, and the famous historical figure, the priest Saigyō looking at Mount Fuji.

2. Martin Foulds, "Zeshin's Life and Works," in *The Art of Shibata Zeshin: The Mr. and Mrs. James E. O'Brien Collection at the Honolulu Academy of Arts* (Honolulu: Honolulu Academy of Arts, 1979), p. 20.

3. The *ema* of *Devil Woman*, see ibid., pls. 204 and 205; Gōke lists thirteen *ema*, p. 169.

4. Ibid., p. 172.

5. Zeshin's *Plant House*, which won the top prize at the First Domestic Exhibition of Business and Industry, was purchased by the Meiji emperor himself. See ibid., pls. 120 and 179. About Zeshin's large-scale works in imperial buildings, see Gōke, p. 77.

6. Gōke, *Shibata Zeshin*, p. 183.

7. Naoteru Uyeno, *Japanese Art and Crafts in the Meiji Era* (Tokyo: Pan-Pacific Press, 1958), p. 111.

8. Zeshin's works collected by Fenollosa and Bigelow are now in the Museum of Fine Arts, Boston.

Cat. nos. 52, 53

1. Kōzō Yoshida, ed., *Hamada Shōji, Gendai Nippon Tōgei Zenshū,* vol. 7 (Tokyo: Shūeisha, 1981), p. 89.

2. Hiroshi Mizuo, *Gendai no Tōgei,* vol. 3 (Tokyo: Kodansha, 1975), p. 151.

3. This contradictory situation also appeared in Europe, where the production of truly utilitarian ware for the ordinary mass population had to depend on a few rich patrons.

4. The bottle is accompanied by the original wooden box, bearing Hamada's signature, that came with the piece when Horiuchi, the donor's father, purchased the piece.

5. This piece was presented to Miss Uchida who spent some time in Japan on a Ford Foundation grant. She has translated Kawai's *Inochi no Mado* (We Do Not Work Alone).